Leadership Development for Public Service

Leadership ☼ Development
for Public Service

Barry A. Passett

President
Systems for Change, Inc.

 Gulf Publishing Company

Book Division · Houston

This book is part of a series of books supported by the American Society for Training and Development as part of its continuing program to encourage publication in the field. Most of the authors are active in ASTD and have con- tributed to its growth over the years. The Publications Committee of ASTD is a continuing link between the editor and the publisher and the membership.

for

Dora Alexander Passett

and William S. Blech

whom

Alexander William

recalls

Library of Congress Catalog Card Number 70-149755

ISBN 0-87201-428-2

Contents

Foreword

In the United States, we have been prone to draw too hard a line between the private and public sectors. Movement of individuals from private industry to government has been easy. Flow in the other direction has been less than satisfactory. Yet, the government now influences much more of our lives than almost any organization in the private sector, including our industrial giants.

As citizens, as taxpayers, as residents of the many jurisdictions in this country—we are all concerned with the quality of the service for which we are paying. Yet, too infrequently attention is directed toward the problems of human resource development. When it does occur, it is usually the result of some horrifying breakdown in public service. Witness the increased funds available for training police at the local level since the long hot summers of the late '60s.

For persons involved in the field of human resource development (HRD), the problem becomes even more crucial. There is a vast group of human resource developers active in many government agencies, and yet too little is known of them and what they are doing. Linkages between HRD personnel in the public and private sectors is inadequate. It is hoped that the common experience to be gained from reading this book will enable them to communicate more effectively with each other.

Leonard Nadler
Series Editor

Preface

As New Year's Day, 1970, approached, readers of the *New York Times* and followers of New York Mayor John Lindsay were treated to days of discussion of a "new trend" in the search for top talent to run the nation's largest city. The call was out for professional "managers."

Lindsay had experimented with the program experts—which is what many say the Eisenhower administrative philosophy was all about. He had also tried the young generalists who had given so much verve to the Kennedy administration. He had tried to stay away from the friends and political allies whose presence, even in relatively small numbers, had been hallmarks of the Truman and Johnson administrations.

In addition, the first Lindsay administration had been marked by a number of managerial innovations at the city level. These changes were designed to raise the caliber of municipal administration by attracting people at the top of the fields, by providing (through the pulling together of departments into superagencies) both broader managerial scope and a more effective distribution of responsibilities and resources, and by giving the mayor stronger policy control. Obviously, the structural and personnel innovations had not meshed. The mayor was going with the structure and altering his recruiting system.

But what was the "professional manager" he was seeking? How would a recruiter know one when he saw one?

The first choice, said to be the harbinger of the new trend, was for Health Services Administrator. It was a surprise at first: a non-physician in a city noted for its credentials consciousness and professionalism. The choice was a deputy administrator for management of the elephantine Human Resourses Administration, a career government servant whose experience had been mostly at the federal level. That experience would appear relevant but somewhat inadequate to a businessman comfortable with private sector definitions of management and development of management competence. The new administrator had served in a series of program development and policy jobs—in the Equal Employment Opportunities Commission, the White House staff and the State Department overseas—which had little to do with the deployment and supervision of large numbers of human and machine resources.

That choice was a surprise. The next was a shock. Who did the mayor choose to pull together perhaps the most politically sensitive agency of all, the Environmental Protection Administration, responsible for garbage and snow removal and improvement of New York's polluted water and air? A young lawyer, a professional politician, with no administrative experience.

As urban problems and people problems dominate the American consciousness, new styles of leadership and administration are required. How have today's trends influenced the requirements?

This questioning stimulated the idea for a specific book on leadership development for public service. Leonard Nadler encouraged its development. He suggested that the primary audience be the training and development professional, particularly in the private sector. My current status as a businessman succeeds ten years of local and federal government service and managing training for community leadership at the state and regional levels. Thus, I seek to place this argument before community leaders and government officials as well. The challenge of a more effective public service is a challenge to the leadership and management capability of people in government. This challenge cannot be translated into an "efficiency" argument which concentrates solely on reducing public expenditures. Cost-cutting rhetoric itself has been a cheap feature of the political din since before the American Revolution, let alone before television. The challenge does mean a new concentration on *people* in public service. Ten years ago, Douglas McGregor summed up the new people-oriented trends in industry in *The Human Side of Enterprise.* Hopefully, before the 1970s pass, someone will be able to write a comparable work on the newly emerging human side of government.

In this attempt to set the stage for such a work, I have had the stimulation of a number of persons whose contributions are noted through the book. Leonard Nadler has been a provocative and helpful guide. My secretary, Mrs. Amie Boyd, had dutifully and efficiently followed through on the typing and production, from the first glimmer to the final version. And most importantly, my wife, Margery, was forebearing, understanding and helpful throughout the process.

Barry A. Passett

November 1970

Leadership
Development
for Public Service

1. The Leadership Gap

A serious gap exists in the performance of public service programs in the United States. The Nixon administration has made clear that the gap is one between promise and performance in large-scale public programs. The gap is attributed to faulty conceptualization and chaotic administration on the implementation side. While there are many arguments with this analysis, particularly from those who held positions of responsibility in prior administrations or who helped develop the programs, there is agreement that performance needs improvement. The thesis here is that training and related human development efforts can lead to much of that improvement.

To the private foundations, whose demonstration projects helped initiate many of the new public programs, the performance gap is often considered one of *leadership*. To socially aware industrialists, who also contributed to such large-scale social innovations as the Job Corps and the Elementary and Secondary Education Act, it is a *management* gap. Some industrialists are familiar with good management and find it lacking in the thickets of civil service and uncertain bureaucratic authority.

Perhaps most significantly, to the recipients of public services there is a gap of *communications* and *commitments,* a gap in delivery as opposed to promise, and a significant gap of involvement.

There are weaknesses on both the managerial and leadership sides. If we stress formal organization in the definition of a manager —a person occupying a position in a formal organization who is responsible for the work of at least one other person or who has formal authority over him—we can see that the traditional weaknesses of government bureaucratic organization apply. If we define a leader as one who is responsible for others not only in formal organizational goals but also individual goals we see that there is a weakness here as well.

Peter Drucker and others have pointed to the manager's entrepreneurial function. John Corson relates that function on the public side to the engineering of a consensus—among exective departments, constituency groups, the legislature—to achieve a goal in the public interest. Corson and Paul estimate that a federal program manager spends perhaps 60 percent of his time "applying the so-called *command skills* of direction, staffing, controlling, planning, and evaluating." He spends a good deal of the rest trying to persuade those over whom he has no control to his point of view. (Corson and Paul, p. 43.)

Since the grant-in-aid program concept became the normal intergovernmental mechanism, significant public programs have been legislated and promulgated at the national level. Then, in keeping with the federal tradition and American dedication to pluralism, these programs have been delegated to state, local and private entities for implementation. John W. Macy, Jr. has called this the policy of "forced change," policy preceding technology and capability.

It worked on the atom bomb and the moon shot and the highway program. When it comes to programs with complex social content, the great hopes and the momentum generated by the forces attempting to fulfill those hopes appear to be dashed. Half of the nearly 400 federal grant-in-aid programs which now put some $15-20 billion dollars into state and local systems each year were enacted in the 1964-1966 period. The programs do not seem to work out as was expected or planned. The managers cannot seem to make public housing, urban renewal, anti-poverty or education of the disadvantaged work to meet their originally stated objectives.

As John Bebout told Senator Muskie's Subcommittee on Inter-governmental Relations in 1965, ". . .there is no greater need at the state and local level than the need for an increase in the input of knowledge and technical competence in policy development and program administration." (*Hearings on Intergovernmental Coopera-tion Act*, p.273.)

In a 1966 article, Dean Stephen K. Bailey stated:

Despite the demands of the war in Vietnam, the critical shortage is not money but people to carry out the programs and effective administrative machinery. Neither Medicare nor aid to education nor the poverty program has either of these at the moment. (Bailey, p.16.)

And writing about "The Why, How and Whence of Manpower Programs" in 1969, Garth Mangum noted succinctly, "The high costs of incompetence are only beginning to be recognized. Authorization has been given, but no program launched, to develop executive leadership and to train for staff capability." (*Annals*, September, 1969, p. 55.)

Frank Sherwood has pointed out some useful supporting information in the data gathered on the first group of executives in the Federal Executive Institute in late 1968. That group of top-level federal managers averaged 48 years in age. Half had last been in school before 1949 and the TV era. Half had no more than one "major" training program in an average 22 years of federal service. Some 40 percent had shifted from the role of technical expert to that of manager as they climbed the ranks. Nearly three-quarters had started new programs or organizations. In a 1969 speech, Sherwood noted, "Yet with relatively little training and limited educational background, it is not clear how they prepared themselves for their management responsibilities and even broader leadership obligation."

David B. Walker of Senator Muskie's staff, referring to the useful survey work of the International City Managers Association, re-ported that less than one-third of local governments regularly sponsor post-entry training for their officials. No city in America has anything approaching a model training program for local officials. Only a few states—California, New York and Michigan being the leaders—have training programs for top management in state departments and agencies. (Golembiewski and Cohen, p. 54.)

Meanwhile, technological advances continue to outpace the ability of city governments to apply their development to full and effective use, as the National League of Cities has been pointing out for years. While cities strain to reach the first generation, computer manufacturers perfect fourth-generation equipment. Skilled people who might apply technology to public administration are working elsewhere.

The living classics of the unmanaged and over-administered bureaucratic nightmare are the urban school systems. They have been executive and political disaster areas, of course, for decades, as a number of books attest. A recent understated view of the New York City schools follows:

> Indeed, this is a system that is strangled in red tape; mired in inertia, incompetence and petty corruption; inefficient; insulated from its clients and from most outside institutions; and fragmented into power blocs that veto new ideas and prevent the efficient use of resources by failing to coordinate. It is leaderless; it has no adequate auditing, monitoring, or information system to evaluate programs and see if policies are carried out; it faces continued subversion of headquarters directives for change by field officials; it protects mediocrity through outdated civil service standards;. . . it is then accountable to nobody but itself. (Rogers, p.28.)

All in all, a pleasant place to work. The Rogers account goes on, making the Peter Principle look like a pleasant metaphor when applied to this reality.

It would be unfair and unwise for us to deal at length with the schools, however. They are too far along the road to disaster for any internal program of leadership development. Unlike most other human services institutions of government, they are probably not amenable to internal change. Public education will continue to blame its failures on the product and will get away with it—until there is much more political muscle mobilized for positive change than was the case in the 1960s. Americans probably need a few more years of squabbling about fluoridation, sex education, sensitivity training, pornographic books and even racial integration before they get down to the more basic problems of educational quality. At that point, questions of leadership development will be extremely relevant.*

The combination of encapsulation in a closed system and poor management is endemic in the executive strata of other public services as well. Law enforcement agencies are a second typical example. Unlike the urban schools, however, there is *some* evidence that they can be managed to achieve public purposes relatively effectively.

Of course, there are many "causes" for the weakness in implementing public programs. The weaknesses begin with the misallocation of national priorities, where war and the extravagant concern for the technology of defense take a disproportionate amount of the federal tax dollar. This misallocation leads not only to a lack of adequate financial resources for programs designed to help people, but also means that management talent follows the path of highest priority.

Mitchell Sviridoff makes the point crisply in the Ford Foundation's 1969 Annual Report (p. 19.). He points out the move to

*An example of blowing in the wind in this field was reported in the *New York Times* of September 29, 1970: "A consortium of five universities has begun a federally funded experimental program to recruit candidates from other professions for training as public school administrators." Ohio State University was taking the lead in this low-volume, high-quality two-year fellowship program. The OSU planners admitted that "one of the major problems in making the program effective might be the reluctance of the educational administrations to open the doors to people from outside the system." Yet they hoped to make the doors open. The next person not trained as a school teacher who becomes superintendent (for more than a token period) of a major urban school system will be the first.

reliance on local and state capability since the 1930s and to the continuing national priority on defense spending and the war in Vietnam:

> Funding aside, there are other reasons for disappointment and failure. They are primarily of an administrative and organizational nature: the proliferating, uncoordinated thicket of Federal bureaucracies and grant-in-aid programs; the lack of experience, authority and talent in local and state governments; insufficient rewards for administrators of hazardous programs; failure to plan comprehensively for use of limited resources; and the difficulty of devising regional approaches within a fragmented governmental structure.

Describing the community action of the 1960s as one technique for reforming social institutions, he later pointed out five other major methods for change and growth in the bureaucracies:

1. Reorganization of established agencies
2. Decentralization
3. PPBS and other rational systems
4. New blood and new careers
5. Strong new administrators (Sviridoff, *PSSR*, 10 October 1968, pp. 5-7.)

Warren Bennis and others have talked about the contemporary organization's need for a peculiar kind of climate and setting. The key word is collaboration. A public executive works in a milieu where he must sell every day: his superiors on needs, the legislature for the tools, his. peers in other agencies on jurisdiction, his subordinates on productivity. He depends upon a collaborative climate where interaction can be directed toward productive social goals.

Obviously, he needs a flexible and adaptive structure. (Just as obviously, in the public sector he is unlikely to get it.) That structure must utilize individual talents, not stifle them. Goals must be clear and agreed upon down through the organization. With generational and political/ideological layers, goal-setting means a process in which people participate to some extent. If they do not, the most noble objectives may be sabotaged down the line. (See Cahn and Passett, pp. 1-64.)

Standards of cooperation, trust, and openness would help to assure that people in public service look upon themselves as truly interdependent. Leaders will not have to fly alone but could negotiate more effectively within their own organizations and among confluent organizations. Since most rewards in public service traditionally have been intrinsic, a conscious recognition of this fact—even in the face of union militancy—can be moved into a system of identifying opportunities for individual autonomy, participation in decision making and other strong portions of "Theory Y" management.

The group synergy which would result should be similar to that which has characterized high-morale public service enterprise using different norms: New Haven city government in the 1950s, the NASA moonshot team, the first two years of the Alliance for Progress and the Peace Corps.

Government Executives

The trend has already begun for executives at the federal, state and local levels to become the mobile, interchangeable, temporary systems managers that so characterizes the modern areas of the private sector. This trend can be expected to accelerate with profound results on traditional leadership development for public service. Managers can no longer expect to spend a career within a single agency, focused on a specific functional area. A man who starts his career as an engineer at NASA may well continue a few years later by becoming a supervisor in the Department of Transportation, move to a state planning department and later switch to an environmental protection agency. Artificial barriers are erected against such flexibility of service, but talented executives are doing it in any event.

More generally, the manager of a public program, particularly among "people programs," has a broad *societal responsibility*. His program should involve large groups of people and make a positive impact on many individuals.

Second, at the same time, he is a *member* of a government, an administration, a team. Students of administration have shown how the programs people want (and have voted for when they elect candidates at all levels) can be sabotaged by administrators who see a primary loyalty to self, profession or dogma beyond the political context. President Kennedy found the "bureaucrats" unwilling to play on his team in 1961; President Nixon had similar problems in 1969.

In the future, the public executive will be different. He will have to be different. He will come from a generation with more, broader and higher education. He will have more than one specialty.

At the same time, like the corporate manager he resembles (and sometimes is), he will be more mobile. The process of going up the ladder a grade at a time is already being replaced by the executive interchange process. If the Intergovernmental Personnel Act gets support and works, the manager will be able to move among the levels of government without loss of status or benefits.

He will have new tools at his command—computer programming, PPBS, systems analysis and others just being introduced into domestic "people" programs.

Clearly, the new government executive will undergo a continuous process of training and education.

At a third level, the executive is *manager* of his own team, his subordinates, in his organization. If his managerial skills are weak, he may not be able to deliver. If they are particularly strong, he may be able to fight his way out of the web and deliver extraordinarily high-quality public service. And, not the least, the manager has *himself* to think about: his career, his mobility, his family, his youthful dreams.

Conscious leadership development can help at all four levels to make the kind of public executives who are credits to the country, the administrations they serve, the people who work with them, and themselves.

2. The Leader: Definitions

There have been many efforts to describe leadership and managerial functions. One moves from sociology and psychology to political science to business administration to personnel to counseling to social psychology and back around the spectrum of disciplines. The semantics differ. Word definitions become tricky. Much of the practical research (case studies, simulations) in recent years has been done at two ends of the scale: top-level national leadership, often with "great man" biases (DeGaulle, Kennedy, Churchill), and industrial management, since there is a market and a payoff there. There certainly has been little study of the training needs of public managers. Any case study of behavior and needs in large organizations is dangerous—the results may upset the rhythm of the power struggle which characterizes so many management groups.

We still do not know very much about leadership. The languages of the disciplines are not easily translated. We confuse various types of leadership: the attribute of a position, the characteristic of a person, a category of behavior. (Katz and Kahn, p. 301) Gordon Lippitt divides our thinking about leadership into four interacting schools:

1. *Traits:* Leaders have a different psychological make-up from other people (the General Patton story).
2. *Situations:* The situation determines which mix of traits and capabilities works ("Put Speaker McCormack in private life and no one would ever notice him").
3. *Functions:* Leaders plan and initiate, provide information and advice, make decisions and provide symbolic ("kingship") imagery.
4. *Birth or fate:* Leaders are "great men" who are born that way and make history. (Lippitt, pp. 83-85.)

Leadership behavior in public organizations moves toward achievement of goals on the one hand and maintenance or strengthening of the organization on the other. The technology of government services is peculiarly relevant, especially in the human services areas, and technology circumscribes leadership roles. In such organizations, the classic production functions—inputs, through-puts and outputs—are expressed in terms of words or human relations. The production inputs (materials and energies directly related to product-oriented work) and maintenance inputs (energy and information necessary to hold people in the system and persuade them to carry out their tasks) are closely related—but may conflict. A leader will recognize that people's roles in the organization are maintained by (1) the demands of the task, (2) the shared values, and (3) the observance of rules. (Katz and Kahn, pp. 454-455.) He will recognize that his organization has a technological system and a work organization (or social) system, each of which places limits on the other. (Rice, p. 4.)

Douglas McGregor emphasized that the prerogatives of power come about not simply through incumbency of office nor from consent by subordinates, but by a collaborative process of goal attainment. In government, success may often be achieved when the job requirements, the parameters within which both leader and followers must work, are set by the situation.

A leader needs some political leeway in which to act. Then he can openly acknowledge interdependence with his subordinates, involve them in setting realistic goals which they can meet col-laboratively, and move to integrate the productive requirements of the total organization with the more immediate needs of the people who man it. (Guest, p. 122.) But two problems intervene: First, a governmental executive, probably faced with short tenure and usually squeezed by many more rigid situational requirements than his private counterpart, may have to place his personal requirements and needs into a shorter time frame; they, therefore, may appear more intense. Second, the public work group itself is a vital organ-izer, to be used and enhanced not only for its productivity but also to reduce the alienation and anomie characteristic of all large bureaucratic organizations and certainly of American government. Alienated groups of public servants cannot provide "connected" services to people.

The questions of reciprocal limits and of the organic nature of the work group interact.

An example here: The administrator of one of New York's human services superagencies came up against the work organization system in his agency relatively early. He wanted to fire several managers whom he felt were impeding progress. A "black con-sciousness" had developed among black employees. Most employees supported the informal system this consciousness created. The managers in question indicated that there would be direct action against the administrator (in picketing, sit-in or other form) if black managers were let go. The administration decided to go slowly and let the situation evolve. A compromise worked itself out over several months. People were shifted; some were let go; a couple moved to find good jobs outside. In all cases, black managers were replaced by black managers. The work of the administration was not seriously disrupted.

The various styles or traits of leadership must be related to group maintenance and goal achievement in a specific context at a specific time. Will the leader initiate? Will he advise? Will he make the deci-sions? Will he be a symbol of stability? Will each individual in the work group do some of each? Will the group process control? The mix among autocratic, laissez-faire and democratic styles is usually strongly determined by the situation—including circumstances outside the work organizational system itself.

Each stage of an organization's development—creation, early survival, stabilization, earning a good name, achieving usefulness and earning respect—requires a different set of knowledge, skills and attitudes. (Lippitt, p. 95.) This developmental concept means that leaders either develop, are replaced, or destroy the organization's capacity for growth.

Public service leadership is political. To return to earlier examples, the Health Services Administrator or the Human Resources administrator is chosen by the mayor. His organizational goals are part of a city-wide strategy. Often that strategy, however vague, will require tradeoffs between optimum management of his administration and the goals of some other department. The "glue" is not output or profits but votes—the quadrennial exercise of a franchise. Most voters will not know whether a government agency was well managed or not. They will get almost no help from the press. There are no "profits." In the early 1960s, the Agency for International Development was perhaps one of the best led and managed of government agencies. During that same period, it was excoriated by the press and Congress and ultimately emasculated. No one agreed on the goals and, therefore, neither did they agree on the "product" any more.

The rewards for effective leadership and management in public service are often inequitable.

Alexander George has gone further in pointing out that a mayor's priority task in urban reform "is no longer merely one of altering and renovating the physical topography of the city, but of participating in and providing encouragement for efforts to preserve and extend democratic values." (George, p. 1196.)

George recalled Richard Neustadt's thesis that the President's power and influence are highly unstable commodities and, following Robert Dahl, applies them "in even greater measure" at the city level:

Studies of successful leaders in urban systems have led to the formulation of a simple, but incisive mode of the "political entrepreneur"—a political activist adept at accumulating a variety of political resources and using them to gain influence and additional resources. To the political entrepreneur who possesses skill and drive, the pluralistic dispersion and fragmentation of power in democratic systems offer unusual opportunities for pyramiding limited initial resources into a substantial political holding. (*Ibid*., p. 1197.)

Mayors Richard C. Lee of New Haven, John Lindsay of New York and John Collins of Boston have been models for this concept.

Yet the small number of models indicates something significant about leadership for public service in America. John Gardner and David McClelland, among others, have described educated Americans' ambivalence about the exercise of power and use of leadership. It has been clear that most university programs for public service careers turn out staff members for leaders, not leaders themselves. Any new system of training and development must address directly the opportunity of power and help reduce cultural drag among the trained toward the use of power.

3. The Issue Develops

For the optimists who hold that American policymakers deal with problems twenty years after the problems ripen, leadership development still runs behind schedule. Every five years or so, the "management gap" is made a major issue. A symbolic action is taken, and the issue subsides.

The first Hoover Commission in the '40s dealt with government management in general, reflecting the new complexity of administration that came with both major technological and social programmatic innovations. John Corson set the stage in 1952 for the Eisenhower changes in government management with a strong plea in his book, *Executives for the Federal Service.* Corson emphasized the differences between private and public leadership. He stressed that public executives must think in terms of public policy and anticipate its effects, keep the public interest first, and have a good knowledge of public relations. The Society for Personnel Administration called for a "Federal Administrative Staff College" in 1953. The second Hoover Commission mentioned needs for executive development.

The Brookings Institution picked up the gauntlet and conducted a number of studies during the Eisenhower years. The Ford Foundation financed Brookings's conferences for federal executives beginning in 1957. The studies were summarized by Marver Bernstein in

1958 in *The Job of the Federal Executive.* Bernstein concentrated on structure and said little about training. In that year, however, the Congress moved. As Leonard Nadler notes, "Officially, training for government employees was not legitimized until 1958 by the passage of the Government Employees Training Act (GETA)." (In Smith, et. al., p. 328.)

GETA provided federal executives with the authority to use their program funds to train employees, using both government and nongovernment resources. It has been used primarily by the Department of Defense, NASA, and the Federal Aviation Administration for in-house (80 percent) training of relatively low-level employees (95 percent to GS-12 level and below).

At the local level, the Municipal Manpower Commission concluded in 1962 that "the quality of APT (administrative, professional and technical) personnel in local governments today, by and large, is inadequate to cope with present and especially emerging metropolitan problems." Wallace Sayre added in the same report:

> In local governments, the executives are unable to exercise effective leadership in personnel policy and practice, the career services are overspecialized and inhospitable to new entrants at the middle or upper ranks, there is insufficient emphasis upon the talents of innovation and creativity, and there is a failure to gain recognition and high prestige for the public service. (*Hearings on Intergovernmental Cooperation Act*, p. 114.)

During this period, another aspect of the failure to develop people for public service was being explored by the Harlem-based team which was to produce the HARYOU plan, *Youth in the Ghetto,* published in 1964. The HARYOU social scientists pointed up the exclusion of blacks from government leadership positions, particularly those whose programs impinged on the black community. Kenneth Clark, Cyril Tyson, Kenneth Marshall and the others who worked on *Youth in the Ghetto* talked about the development of a "community action institute," which would train ghetto residents for public service leadership.

Also in this period came the focus for congressional activity in the area of upgrading the skills and competence of government managers. Senator Edmund Muskie and his Subcommittee on Intergovernmental Relations of the Senate Committee on Government Operations has been the legislative center for dealing with the question. As is customary, Senator Muskie as chairman has had the major responsibility for the work of the subcommittee.* Through the Kennedy and Johnson administrations, he shepherded the legislation which was to become the Intergovernmental Cooperation Act of 1968 and went on to lay the groundwork for an Intergovernmental Personnel Act. These pieces of legislation—helped along by the good staff work of men like David B. Walker, Edwin Webber and E. Winslow Turner** and by the support of the ranking minority senator, Karl Mundt—provide the critical legislative infrastructure for a developmental approach to public service personnel policy. While not yet providing the money to do a significant job through the mechanisms in the legislation itself, they have provided the legal and policy backdrop for new initiatives in leadership development for public service.

The Intergovernmental Personnel Act, which passed the Senate twice (as of late 1970) and was shelved in the House, was caught in a rather typical bind. Representative Edith Green, who heads the Special Subcommittee on Education of the House, had an Education for the Public Service proposal included as Title IX of the Higher Education Act. This title was designed to channel professionally trained persons into public service, but it received little support from the administration, and its appropriations have been miniscule. It works on the basis of a state plan funneled through state departments of education, a process highly favored by Mrs. Green. The main conflict over the Intergovernmental Personnel Act appears to

---

* Other Senators with at least five years of service on the Subcommittee include Sam Ervin, Jr., Abraham Ribicoff and Karl Mundt.

**Turner had personal experience in trying to get innovative grant-in-aid programs off the ground. His concern for quality performance was reflected in the years of hard labor required to move the legislation through the Senate.

be over that mode of administration: If the governors were to receive the funds and control the programs, the urban interest groups and congressmen would not be interested in it. The problem of an appropriate local option provision, as proposed in the Senate bill, was due for resolution late in 1970 or 1971.*

The Muskie Subcommittee's work had turned up interesting data by 1967. The senator pointed out that the great public service growth since 1946 has been in state and local government, up from some 3.3 million to over eight million, with the curve still going up. Their recruiting needs are over a quarter of a million administrative, professional and technical people a year. Civilian federal employment remained relatively stable in these 20 years. State and local civil governmental manpower now accounted for 80 percent of the total; but, as the senator explained in a speech supporting the Intergovernmental Personnel Act, "The striking fact is that this growth in manpower and public programs at state and local governmental levels has not been accompanied by improvement in the quality and professional caliber of administration." (Hearings, *op. cit.*, p. 190.)

Muskie adduced other data, including some pulled together for President Johnson's May, 1966, speech at Princeton University, which was the major presidential treatment of the leadership gap. These included:

1. Approximately half the nation's municipal health directors will be eligible for retirement within the next 10 years.
2. Two vacancies exist for every graduate of a university course in city or regional planning.

Even more important, he quoted the concerns of Elliot L. Richardson (now Secretary of HEW) about low expectations among prospective applicants for having "satisfactory professional expe-

---

*For the text of the key debate on the Senate bill, passed in late 1969, see Appendix A. The House bill was reported out of committee in 1970 and passed in the waning hours of the 91st Congress.

riences" in public service. Richardson pointed to the "low image" of the state civil service in Massachusetts as the most important single factor in discouraging college students from applying for professional, technical or administrative positions.

The Committee on Economic Development had a long-standing interest in more efficient government management. By 1964, they were ready to issue a report with major recommendations for change. It was called "Improving Executive Management in the Federal Government." They began by describing the difficulty of the public executive's job, the varied constituencies and the different performance standards. They clearly agreed that there are no objective yardsticks for managerial excellence.

CED's definition of the problem was eloquent but not too specific:

> Narrowly conceived, development includes a variety of training efforts both on and off the job; more broadly, it is the complex process of accumulating the skills, attitudes, knowledge, and experience essential to produce performance of the highest order. . . .

> Leading private corporations spend large sums each year on manpower training, with executive development one of the principal aims. They have found that to have sound management they must plan and prepare for it consciously, through training and developing those selected for. . . managerial responsibility. (CED, p.35.)

The CED report went on to make recommendations which still seem radical six years later. For example, every "professional" person should be required to take management training before he takes a line post. While this thought is familiar in military and scientific circles, it has never been applied to the "soft" programs.

CED suggested that the federal government should perhaps establish its own management training institution (in addition to the Kings Point Executive Seminar and the war colleges). CED called for the creation of an Office of Executive Personnel in the White House to handle classification, recruitment, training, development, and separation for all supergrade positions. The Committee recommended that this office run orientation programs for all high-level federal executives.

This report received fairly wide circulation. CED followed up with further recommendations in its 1966 report "Modernizing Local Government."

Yet, in the Winter, 1970, issue of *The Public Interest*, (pp. 50-51) Robert C. Wood* could offer the following peroration to his article on "When Government Works":

Building effective government in the United States is not a challenge for which there are simple answers. Giving tasks back to states, localities, and neighborhoods, in the hopes of reducing them to manageable proportions, is not a self-evident solution—not until the resources and motives of these institutions are appraised. Building up presidential staffs, in the expectation that they can think, act, lead, and manage may be necessary but is far from sufficient. With operations flowing increasingly to the top and policy covertly bootlegged in at the bottom, the dilemma can be resolved only by a systematic series of steps which extends proper presidential oversight throughout the executive branch, encourages operational discretion at the program level, and rewards professional behavior.

The plain fact is that this country has never been serious about establishing a responsible and responsive bureaucracy. Still captivated by the revolutionary effort to tame a king's power; still misquoting Lord Acton, and implying power encourages corruption rather than rectitude; still regarding the delivery and nondelivery of a particularly public service as a scene in a morality play, the American government has relied heavily on the energies and the devotion of the organization amateur. The political lawyer who has suddenly been asked to handle administrative matters in the White House; the academic economist called on to weld together the energies and loyalties

*Wood retired from the Undersecretary's job at HUD in 1969 to the banks of the Charles, where he took Daniel P. Moynihan's chair as director of the Harvard-MIT Joint Center for Urban Studies and then moved on to the presidency of the University of Massachusetts.

of a large number of men; the neighborhood leader introduced into participatory programming; the government engineer or accountant asked to grow into leadership—these have been the executors of our public policy.

This country possesses policies and programs that are clearly capable of remedying many of our paralyzing ills if only they are well-executed; it cannot afford amateurs in administration any longer. We cannot will government away; we cannot endure a second-rate government; we cannot solve problems by rhetorical denunciations. We must at long last take the problem of public management seriously.

At the same time (February, 1970), a university team financed by the Connecticut Research Commission reported on the steadily growing shortage of "urban generalists."

The study team, headed by Professor Bruce Esposito of the University of Hartford, reported that "at all levels—state, regional and local—agencies of both the governmental and semi-governmental 'action' structure have committed themselves to programs for meeting visible needs. Yet all agencies appear to be hampered by a lack of adequate staff properly trained to meet the wide range of demands placed upon them."

The Connecticut shortage: a minimum "demand" for 200 urban generalists. The principal skill needed for success is "the ability to manipulate people."

The study pointed out that current training programs were too narrow and removed from practical urban experience. College degrees were not relevant. The skills the team listed in order of importance as being necessary by current practitioners were:

1. Communicates
2. Manages day to day work
3. Sensitive to people's needs, community life styles.
4. Utilizes good human relations practices
5. Designs realistic programs needed in an urban setting
6. Knows sources of financial aid
7. Plans economic or social systems of an urban structure

8. Plans physical layout
9. Researches information, including analysis and formulation of statistical procedures
10. Discerns the unity of a city or urban structure.

The present practitioners emphasized interpersonal and political manipulation skills. They agreed that administrative skills are secondary—management, research and statistics, planning and programming.*

The Hartford study built on more general data gathered by University of Pittsburgh researchers in 1969. They found "19 fields or functions for which trained administrative and professional personnel are vital to the development of suitable conditions in the nation's urban areas." These are:

General management of urban governmental and service agencies
Administrative staff functions: budgeting, finance, personnel, administrative management, legal counsel
Urban and regional planning
Urban development and renewal
Housing management
Community action and opportunity development
Industrial-economic development
Public works engineering and administration
Urban transportation
Administration of regulatory programs, safety, and justice
Social service and public welfare
Employment-social security
Community recreation and parks
Environmental health**

* This account is based on information in *Community Development*, February, 1970, p. 9.

**Ron Linton, in his book *Terracide* (Boston: Little Brown, 1970) and elsewhere, makes a strong case for a priority for human resource development in the environmental field.

Hospitals
Education planning and administration
Public library service
Administration of culture and the arts
Teaching and research in these fields. (See *Hearings, Intergovernmental Personnel Act,* p. 156.)

Dean Donald Stone concluded that in only five of these fields had significant support to provide the necessary educational underpinning been authorized: public health, social welfare, educational planning and administration, public library service and some aspects of law enforcement. And many would argue that even some of these five were being shortchanged.

4. Creative Pressures for the '70s

While there has always been a gap between need and perform-ance in leadership development activities, the current crisis in American society makes the gap much less tolerable.

Public service opportunities must be opened to meet the "revolu-tions" of the 1970s. The federal government, and to a comparable extent, local and state governments, were made aware in the '60s of their ingrained patterns of exclusion and discrimination against blacks. Of course, large numbers of blacks had federal careers before this time—mostly in the Post Office, where politics has controlled and discrimination assured that they were not given equal develop-ment and advancement opportunities. Some compensatory pro-grams, focused either on hiring or training or both, were initiated. The most telling came in the anti-poverty areas. Because much of the clientele of OEO and Department of Labor programs was expected to be black, black executives were recruited by the dozens and young blacks were given attractive offers to enter public service or to move to the new agencies. In some cases, training was provided on the job. Internship programs sprang up as well.

The black revolution coincided with a burst of union organizing activity in public service at all levels of government. Teachers, post-men, hospital workers—even the scorned Foreign Service officer—

picketed, shouted and negotiated their way through grievances. Many engaged in such militance for the first time. In many cases, grievances had little to do with wages and were more directly related to quality of life and personal fulfillment issues.

Just as labor militance and the Wagner Act in the 1930s were the motive forces behind industrial management's new concern with management as an act of dealing with people, so the new militance has pulled the rug off of government management's extraordinary weakness. The Civil Service system, at all levels, with its stylized procedures and creaky machinery, had disguised the antiquated management practices in government. When managers have to deal with militants, particularly those organized into unions, the weaknesses of the system (and their own training) become apparent.*

The country now faces at least three additional claims to equality in employment and managerial competence. Each will strain current capability to provide leadership development services. Each will require at least as significant a change in the amount of service required and the style in which it is offered as has the black revolution. These new claims come from "the ethnics," women and youth.

The Ethnics

Following on the heels of "black power" came "Puerto Rican power" and "Chicano power." In the public service, black power was accommodated much the way the earlier immigrant groups with newly potent political clout had been. In big cities, New York for example, the Irish often took the police department, the Italians the sanitation department, and the Jews and Irish split the school system. The blacks were "given" community action agencies and sometimes Model Cities Agencies. So were Puerto Ricans and Chicanos in the few cases where their claim to be the dominant minority carried political valence.

*I am indebted to Congressman Frank J. Brasco and Dr. James Watson of Rutgers University for the key connections here.

In the 1970s, however, public service faces a new challenge. In the restatement or reawakening of traditional ethnic politics, a large number of forgotten ethnic groups—backbones of the so-called "silent majority"—are looking for participation. Just as blacks called for (and have been receiving) more black policemen, census takers, welfare workers and social service executives in their neighborhoods, big-city Italian, Polish and Scandanavian groups will be looking for their own in federal, state and local government. The provocative work of Daniel P. Moynihan and Nathan Glazer, in *Beyond the Melting Pot* and later articles, made clear that ethnics went beyond nationality groups. They concluded their 1963 study: "Religion and race define the next stage in the evolution of the American peoples. But the American nationality is still forming: its processes are mysterious, and the final form, if there is ever to be a final form, is as yet unknown." (p. 315.)

In the form of the 1970s, ethnic politics pays off. There will be a continuing demand for more "rising to the top" by various ethnic and even religious groups.

Many working class and lower middle class ethnic neighborhoods, particularly in big cities like New York and Los Angeles, are exhibiting symptoms of alienation and anomie which in the early 1960s were attributed only to black ghettos. The Wallace vote in 1968 was a small indication. More significant, probably, have been the mayoralty elections in dozens of American cities of all sizes, where incumbents with progressive records have either retired or been voted out of office. The strong ethnic vote in the outer boroughs of New York City—in Slavic, Irish and even Jewish neighborhoods—for Major Lindsay's two (Italian-American) opponents in 1969 is another example. Lindsay pulled through, thanks to the split of nearly 60 percent of the votes among his opponents.

The Women

By mid-1970, it was evident that Women's Liberation would make Black Liberation look like a dress rehearsal. One of the key demands of women's groups, now including even the more "conservative" ones, has become equal pay and promotional opportunity for equal work and merit.

Although the record for the federal civil service in this regard is probably better than that of private business, women have long been exploited in government work. Women with credentials equal to those of men at the beginning levels have often been shunted into the secretarial lines. They are too often promoted to jobs which require a great deal of paper work or busywork—and left there, even when their policymaking and executive skills equal those of men. A double edged discriminatory practice common in the government of the '60s was the "twofer" system. A federal executive would split a key technical or administrative job (at, say, the GS-14 level) into two lower level jobs (a GS-7 and a GS-9). He would hire two bright girls not long out of graduate school or college and motivate each to produce twice as much as would be expected from her.

The black revolution initially brought a great many black women up the executive ladder, since they had the professional training and credentials. Their early success has caused a backlash, however, based on sociological interpretations of the so-called dominant role of the female in black society. This backlash has led to a further struggle on the part of black women to find an appropriate role and level of functioning in public service. Since the blacks have come from such a deficit position in terms of public service opportunities, the male-female rivalry probably can be played out over a number of years without a serious need for a winner. In the meantime, however, black females will be under double pressure.

In the future, women will be looking for career advancement opportunities, and for the training necessary to meet them. Even more radical, women who have been working as executive secretaries at all levels of government, seeing the men come and go as fads and administrations change, will more and more demand the opportunity to gain the educational and other credentials which will enable them to get the jobs they know they can do.

The Youth

The black, the ethnic, the female—all come together in the youth revolution. The active search of this generation of educated youth for a more open, honest, uninhibited, participatory, communitarian and idealistic society is already having great impact on public service. The wheeler-dealer, conflict-of-interest business tradition, which "got things done" when translated into the public sector, is under intense fire.

The young people want immediate payoff, in human terms, for work in public service. The Peace Corps and VISTA exploited this idealism. It will be hard to convince a generation accustomed to seeing administration buildings burn that it will take ten years of planning and acquisition before a public housing project can be built or an urban renewal project's construction started.

Young people in government agencies are hip to certain kinds of developmental styles and will work to encourage their utilization. The old film-and-lecture training method is out. As Bennis and Slater point out (p. 86.), the romantic motivation behind demands for sensitivity and encounter training anticipates the new world of temporary systems in public and private life. Yet for young people, the training which emphasizes openness, feedback, immediacy, communication at a feeling level and the like is particularly appropriate to humanizing current bureaucratic systems.

Many more will probably be interested in the human relations of government management and will volunteer for those staff development functions which once were relegated to the "drones in the bowels of the personnel department." A higher level of competence may be brought to bear on training and leadership development activities.

The Environment

The current focus on the fitness of man's environment is a major revolution in thought and a political force of the 1970s. Managers at all levels of government are no more prepared than are mayors, governors or even presidents to deal with the complex problems which concern for the environment implies. Economic systems with no concern for people, other systems whose values were anti-human—all are being tested against the human values asserted by women, young people and ethnics. The environment, too, is being tested. Few asked the state highway administrator in the 1950s if the interstate highway was going to harm the marsh ecology of an area. If property values were considered appropriately, the public works went through. There was no fourth jetport for the New York region in the Great Swamp (near Morristown, New Jersey) not so much because it was an ecological treasure, but because so many rich and powerful New Jerseyans had estates in that area. Airports were placed near big cities and developers were permitted to build houses to the runways' edge, with little concern for noise, fumes, or safety. Automobile travel was encouraged by a variety of federal programs; and the chewing up of the land, willy-nilly, was the outcome of a federal housing subsidy program for suburban developments only.

The Future

These combined revolutions should insure payment of more coherent attention to all forms of leadership development. Job enrichment is becoming more important as a strategy for keeping and moving people. The educational leave is now a part of the federal personnel system and has begun to trickle down to state and local levels. On-the-job training is borrowing more from industry, both in terms of payoff for investment in skills training and of the importance of investment in better human relations.

The interests of the blacks, the ethnics, the women and the young will not always converge on any one issue. But the constant ferment and battle should keep public management's attention focused on things that can be done to increase mobility and reduce tensions.

The public service has only begun to invest in staff development. By 1980, the value of that investment should have multiplied many fold.

A warning note: The emphasis on the revolutions of the 1960s should be seen in the context of leadership development for public service. Obviously, the general tone of the public debate in America is becoming more strident, less rational. The politics of the irrational is now commonplace. At this writing there is far more power in reaction than in all the "revolutions" combined. Since much of the impetus to public service leadership is said to be altruistic and idealistic, *the political climate itself is the major personnel policymaker in government.*

Normally, the upgrading of skills in the government service receive attention during fallow periods in American political life. During activist periods, there is more concern with policy and program, less with structure and institution building.

The current period, therefore, offers a prospect for co-opting blacks, young people, women and ethnics into government, where they then may be put to work in a structured game of stalemate.

5. The Private-Public Dialogue

It might appear that private industry has a better record in on-the-job development of leadership skills and talent than has the public service. It is true that most major training and human development technologies of the past decades were created by university people, tested and applied in industry and then made available to other uses. Sensitivity training, for example, was first tested on teachers, community leaders and ethnic interest groups, but its great burst into growth industry status came after its adoption by a number of major corporations in the late '50s and '60s.

It is interesting to note, however, that when the various levels of government parcel out functions to the private sector, the management gap does not close. While most businesses engaged in government contract work have more freedom to hire and fire than Civil Service provides, experience in such "cost plus" efforts as the Job Corps and military training programs indicates that other challenges to management may be just as serious. (The general rule is that private companies will deliver the minimum product at the highest cost; government operation may not even provide the minimum product, but its costs will be lower.)

The National Alliance of Businessmen's (NAB) effort to find jobs for unemployed minority group workers is a good example of the challenge. The highest levels of corporate management were mobilized to support and lend help to the effort. Adequate government financial backing was pledged.

The goals were kept simple—perhaps too simple. Management was permitted to define new hires. No particular safeguards were built in to assure that business would not use government funds to recruit, train and provide remedial education for workers they would have hired in any case. The subsidy to the private sector was made quite clearly as it was the only carrot available to induce businesses to hire black and other minorities in large numbers in a short time.

The government provided over $300 million for the first three years of the JOBS programs under NAB. While government agencies were to locate and identify the hard-core unemployed, the companies were to provide the training and some placement services. Government funds were for "extras" health, basic literacy and perhaps transportation. Subsidies averaged over $4,000 per person.

Three out of four NAB trainees seem to stick. There is some creaming, in that the large bulk have worked and are between 20 and 40 years of age.

In an early analysis of the program, August Bolino reported that, while the public relations front at NAB was good, the public/private marriage had its limitations. Chrysler ended its joint apprenticeship program with the Department of Labor "convinced they can do the job better by doing it alone." The company found the program too long. Federal standards do not apply in all states. No single educational program could fit several states' requirements. (Bolino, pp. 192-193.) Later reports, during the 1969-70 recession, were more critical. A Greenleigh Associates study said that the JOBS program was far behind its own goals, that most jobs were vulnerable to technological change, that office-oriented work (read *girls*) had the highest employment retention rate, and that the program failed to develop effective links to health, manpower, education and other community programs.

These examples point to gaps in leadership and management in the attempts being made to resolve America's most pressing social problems. Leadership failures are analagous to the horror stories in the business literature: The leader who developed a more efficient method for manufacture of buggy parts in 1905; the euphoria surrounding the birth of the Edsel; miracle leadership at General Dynamics in the '50s.

Ford Motor Company and General Dynamics survived and learned from the experience. They changed leadership, products, systems. OEO may survive, too, as may New York's HRA and state departments of education. Some change was achieved in leadership, systems and programs; but it came by much trial and much error. If we focus on leadership, however, isn't there a better way to run organizations? Is trial by inexperience and charisma a necessity for every innovation?

Should public programs be so well managed that they begin to control their own destinies, overwhelming the less efficient and effective political forces which are supposed to set their policy? Does sloppy management better serve democratic governing principles?

The OEO Case

A case study of leadership gap at the federal level comes out of the history of the Office of Economic Opportunity, created in 1964 to manage the "war on poverty." A complete new structure—federal, state and local—had to be created in a year to conduct a series of functions largely new at each level. R. Sargent Shriver, the first director of the federal office, had a particular problem in executive recruitment: he was a Kennedy in-law in a Johnson administration. Neither the President nor the Congress was about to give him a free hand in staffing his agency. The congressional committee responsible for his money forced him to renege on his own choice for a deputy, Adam Yarmolinsky, who had guided the task force which organized the war on poverty in 1964. The President's responsivesness to Mayor Richard Daley of Chicago made it impossible for Shriver to keep top staff loyal to him in the regional office located in that city, his own supposed political base. With constraints of this variety, it was clear from the beginning that Shriver was not going to have the organizational success which was his three years earlier in the Peace Corps. The development of the Peace Corps began to seem analogous to a go-go mutual fund; OEO resembled a major new hard-goods industry in an already crowded field.

Functionally, OEO had difficulty: at least four different definitions of its role and purpose, according to Daniel P. Moynihan, were accepted at the same time by people outside the office and within it. These included: (1) a Peace Corps model in which OEO was to provide a cadre of enthusiastic people to attack poverty at the local level from outside the establishment; (2) a Budget Bureau model, in which OEO was to coordinate more effectively all local planning and programming related to federal dollars; (3) an Alinsky or conflict model, in which OEO was to "rub raw the sores of discontent" at the local and national levels, mobilizing the poor and powerless for political action; and (4) an improved service-delivery model, in which OEO was to take the current federally financed programs for the poor, experiment with improvements and manage the improved results better. (Moynihan, *passim.*) OEO did not even issue a mission statement or formal statement of goals until it had been in business some three years.

The *structure* through which these varied views of function were to be managed and somehow evolve was itself perplexing. Director Shriver obviously was keeping the question of political support uppermost in his mind. The Job Corps was a means of attracting support from the industrial giants and the land-grant colleges. Many big businesses, such as Litton Industries and ITT's Federal Electric, were willing to run centers on a cost-plus-fixed-fee basis. Some of the major universities were also attracted. VISTA was a means of attracting support from the younger generation and its intellectual campfollowers in the universities and media. The volunteers' program was a natural for TV and press coverage, was relatively non-controversial and could be used as an entering wedge for support of all of OEO.

Job Corps and VISTA, therefore, remained highly centralized operations, reporting to a Washington hierarchy and overseen directly by Shriver and his top management.

OEO's intent was to decentralize the more controversial and hard to define Community Action Program (CAP) early in the game. Grant management was delegated to a series of regional offices. However, the directors of these OEO regional offices had nominal charge of VISTA and Job Corps functions in their regions. They reported directly to Shriver, rather than to Theodore Berry, the Cincinnati lawyer who directed CAP. The CAP staff in the regional offices included a large number of young people, with a larger proportion of minority group members and women in substantial jobs than most government agencies, and probably a smaller proportion of paperwork and financial management experts than most federal agencies normally develop. Local Community Action Program boards and executives, living at the frontlines during a period of acute social unrest and community polarization, had to deal with this federal system. State Economic Opportunity offices, an intermediate layer charged basically with technical assistance functions, also worked through the regional system.

This chaotic managerial situation was made even more complex by the delegation of Economic Opportunity Act functions to other government departments. The principal recipient was the Labor Department, whose implementation system was state-based in the state employment services.

The OEO regional director, therefore, had to handle a complex of relationships at the local, state and interagency levels. He had to manage a staff whose perceptions of the job and loyalties often conflicted with his, each other's and certainly the Washington hierarchy's *realpolitik* views. With his Washington special office colleagues, the OEO regional director had to approve and manage grants amounting to more than a billion dollars a year. Here was a real challenge to his leadership capability and managerial competence.

The Role of the States

At the state level, weakness of adminstration (including that faintness of heart when faced with the offer by private citizens to buy public favors) is so endemic that public confidence in the ability of states to provide service has almost completely eroded.

Nelson Rockefeller's "creative federalism" was a late–'50s approach to the increase of state management ability to match the increased state responsibility. Rockefeller proved that it could work in the field of higher education. His Urban Development Corporation, a pioneer in the housing field, shows great promise. As governor of North Carolina, Terry Sanford tried to carry the concept into the fields of manpower, community development and public education. Despite help from the Ford Foundation and a number of the most innovative programs his state had seen, Sanford could not institutionalize many of his approaches to strengthening the state.

A decade after its coverage by the media, "creative federalism" as it relates to the states found its way onto the national agenda. But can the Nixon administration make the 50 state governments respond? Is there capability to manage things?

The experience under Title I of the Elementary and Secondary Education ACT (ESEA) is not promising. Title I was companion "Great Society" legislation to the Economic Opportunity Act. It was designed to provide assistance to develop new programs and upgrade the level of education received by poor children, so that they might break out of the poverty cycle and take advantage of the opportunities which better education can open. Significantly, the money was channeled through the existing mechanism: allocated to state departments of education who then re-allocated it to local boards of education. The formula was weighted in favor of school districts with the most children from families with incomes under the poverty line. A procedure for involving people to be served in the planning was mandated.

From the beginning it was clear that management of the program was going to be a major problem. After one year of operations, a number of analysts pointed out that the program still had great promise but that the money was not going for the purposes set forth by Congress. Local school boards all over the county were using the money to beef up existing programs, not innovate. They were refusing to "discriminate on behalf of poor children" and were providing services across the board. It was difficult to find educators who could plan programs and evaluate at the local level. Locals given the chance to innovate simply copped out. Rural school districts bought more buses. In Newark, several million dollars just melted into the system, without program or audit.

State department heads were afraid to hold local school boards to the plans that had been submitted. Where they wanted to meet the standards in the act, the hands-off tradition and lack of managerial competence (and political will) at the state level cooled their ardor. The money continued to move. Late in 1969, both an internal HEW report and an external evaluation criticized Title I for failing to make significant specific changes in the educational achievement of poor children.

The Cities

Although the state level is perhaps the most stereotyped in its lack of managerial and leadership talent, it is at the local level that the famine has taken its greatest toll. Most American cities and towns provide an abysmally low quality of services to their residents, particularly when those residents' per capita income is taken into account. From trash collection and street cleaning to health care and child care, other countries with lower living standards have more effective municipal service delivery. (This statement does not imply any anti-American snobbism. No one handles modern traffic effectively. London's air pollution and Leningrad's housing make clear that some problems are endemic to any "modernized" urban society.)

While much of the gap here is due to a lack of resources—a starving of the public sector—the differences in service among American cities and towns indicate that management has a good deal to do with it. New Haven's ability to attract perhaps $300 in federal grants for each of its citizens made it possible to renew its downtown core and its most depressed neighborhoods and to provide exemplary municipal services at the same time. Trenton attracted enough federal and state funds to experiment with almost every educational innovation popular in the literature of the last decade: street academies, Outward Bound, tutorials, English as a second language, etc.

Aggressive, progressive management will pay—but sometimes things do not work out exactly as planned.

In 1966, the newly elected Republican mayor of New York City appointed a task force to determine how best to meet the human resources needs of America's largest and supposedly most ungovernable metropolis. The study group was led by Mitchell Sviridoff, then executive director of Community Progress, Inc., in New Haven, an agency financed by the Ford Foundation and federal grants and considered a model of manpower and community development. Working under Sviridoff were Henry Cohen, who had a long career in New York municipal service and had been a key member of the Wagner administration, and other practical experts in urban affairs. They studied the complexities of New York's welfare, poverty, manpower, community organization, education, addiction, early childhood policy and youth services. (The housing and health spheres were given to other task forces.) Their conclusion was that all of these functions were being inadequately managed, if not mismanaged. Their interdependencies were compelling—yet they existed without central planning, managerial control, or management information systems. The only controls were in the Budget Bureau, the accounting arm of the controller's office, and the mayor's office. The solution would be to pull all of these agencies and their functions into one superagency which might then manage effectively. Welfare's budget and staff were immense—over 80 percent of the whole functional stew. A single agency, *not* called Welfare, might move that Leviathan and permit creation of a truly human-oriented municipal service system.

The mayor accepted the report and created the agency, naming Sviridoff to organize and run it. The new Human Resources Administration contained the renamed Welfare Department, now the Social Services Agency, under a commissioner who reported to the administrator. Other commissioners headed new units: the Community Development Agency, the Manpower and Career Development Agency, the Youth Services Agency and the Addiction Services Agency. A small office of educational liaison was set up to give the administrator some input into the school system.

Sviridoff left after completing the structuring and staffing of the administration in its first year. His successor, Mitchell Ginsberg, moved up from Commissioner of Social Services. Ginsberg had been a professor of social work. He brought in several top officials from the social welfare academic scene. This change in personnel soon became reflected in the policy and orientation of HRA. Social services, or welfare, became dominant, as its budget (but not the initiatives of the reformers) indicated it should. There was little stress on management except in terms of budget control. That emphasis received a blow when it was discovered that over half a million dollars in checks to nonexistent summer Neighborhood Youth Corps enrollees had been stolen. The thieves in the HRA fiscal apparatus had been clever and had exploited political fears over possible riots. Still, the fact was that hundreds of young people supposedly working did not exist.

While politics and clever dishonesty could be blamed for much of the trouble in the Manpower and Career Development Agency, more complex processes seemed to be at work at the Community Development Agency. CDA was charged with dividing the small federal and city anti-poverty pie among the 20 community corporations representing the city's poorest neighborhoods. The agency had developed no standards for the distribution, except for some rough measures of numbers of poor people. There were no performance standards by which to reward or punish. Each corporation, therefore, threw its weight as best it knew: political "in's," picketing, sit-ins, blasts in the papers, etc. The impression to the public was a mixture of chaos, ingratitude, ineptitude and indignation.

There were indications of some impulsiveness as well. Early in the HRA development, the Youth Services Agency disbanded the noteworthy 20-year Youth Board program of street-gang workers. The reasoning: teen-age gangs were no longer a New York problem. Soon thereafter, the Addiction Services Agency called attention to the fact that narcotics addiction was reaching epidemic proportions in the 12-16 age ranges. ASA wanted a street worker staff to deal with the problem.

HRA's general hiring practices were remarkable in a number of ways. Even more than OEO at the federal level, HRA attempted to recruit blacks and Puerto Ricans for a majority of jobs, including managerial, professional, technical and clerical positions. Minority group members were represented at the commissioner level as well as among the deputy administrators. (If Jews are classed among the minorities, at several points 100 percent of top management was "minority.") Blacks and Puerto Ricans in top jobs tended to have backgrounds similar to their colleagues: social service, academic, and more recently, anti-poverty. Moving down through the hierarchies, valuable experience credentials began to fall away. (There is general agreement that *academic* credentials meant as little at HRA in the '60s as they did at Ford Motor Company in the '20s.) For many persons in managerial and technical jobs—faced with the Civil Service hurdle at some point—it was the old white employer's hustle: easy hiring, no training, large responsibility, confused authority. . .which adds up to failure.

Several component agencies, especially the Manpower and Career Development Agency and the Youth Services Agency, made stabs at developing training programs to meet the problem. HRA's central administration threatened for three years to develop a training strategy. Training was sometimes provided on a crash basis before Civil Service exams. Sensitivity, communications and management development labs were run from time to time. Generally, however, the HRA moved into the second Lindsay administration, a change in its own administration and into the 1970s without a coherent internal human resource development system.*

The TRW Example

The example from the private sector most often cited as the model for organization development is TRW Systems, Inc. TRW is said to have resembled a public agency in many ways. Most of its work through the early 1960s was for government clients. It was large, with about 16,000 employees in 1969. Its employees were concentrated in the most modern technical and professional occupations. They were faced with a major change of missions after 1960 (as were such government agencies as the Department of Labor and the Agency for International Development). When they made the move from planning and software (related primarily to the U.S. Air Force's missile gap) into the field of space projects and hardware development, TRW's management identified some key problems. They had to develop management skills in technically oriented

*By late 1970 a new top management team headed by Jule Sugarman had set a high priority on the development of such a system.

people—a problem common to all of America's high-technology endeavors from hospitals to submarines to computer makers and users. All TRW managers had to learn the new, complex and inter-dependent matrix management system. The engineering staff had to keep up with the information flow in their highly technical fields.

TRW management, therefore, faced a network of knowledge, skills and relationships problems similar to those of a major government agency in a period of significant change. They began with a year of planning and of sending small groups of executives to the National Training Laboratories. They then moved into team-building, using T-groups for a dozen managers at a time. During this period, they restructured their entire "personnel" operation to focus on organization development. They matched their staff with outside consultants.

They moved away from off-the-job laboratory training toward more on-the-job training and team-building. Four-hour problem-solving sessions, "sensing" and organizational mirror techniques began to become the dominant mode.

TRW never insisted that executives go to the laboratory training. They worked with those who were ready to work and did not push hard on the others. Even had they been more demanding, it would have been too costly and the trainers capable of handling that large a volume simply were not (and are not) available. As they changed the working environment of the company, they found their need for laboratory training declining. At the same time, they noticed a key result: problems and conflicts were being resolved at lower and lower levels in the organization.

It is important to note that the matrix or project group management system was breaking all the normal pyramidal organizational rules. Each manager's status changed from project to project or phase to phase; he had several different evaluators at all times. It became necessary to add on to the traditional industrial command skills which are superior-subordinate, competitive and impersonal. The add-on was a whole new series of skills: teamwork, including shared responsibility, trust, instant teamwork, joint "ownership" of work by team leader and members; conflict resolution in win/win settings; a good deal of independence and upward influence; and a climate which encouraged helping, asking for and receiving help. This climate was made up of a number of interpersonal growth factors, some of which had been enhanced by the early laboratory training: respect, active listening (empathy), genuineness and openness, congruence, respecting each other's separateness, and confrontation and feedback.

While hard data on the dollar value of the success of this process over ten years is hard to come by, there are some physical indicators: the company remained extremely profitable through a major turnaround in its business, and managers seem to consider it an excellent place to work.

TRW management appears to agree that the organization development program made sense for the well-educated and competent personnel of one high-technology company. They attest to the need for third-party or consultant intervention and for active cooperation between external and internal consultants to put to work in a pragmatic fashion all the data they gather. They agree that such an organization development effort is dependent on top management commitment and involvement, and on integration of the organization development effort with ongoing personnel, industrial relations and other people–related functions.

This account, taken from a 1969 Cornell School of Labor and Industrial Relations workshop, and from conversations with people familiar with the TRW experience, is not presented so much as a statement on what happened in that company. It is more an illustration that management conviction, backed up by money and good people, can bring large organizations into congruence with current thinking about what an organization should be. Young people, women and blacks entering into management roles in government often tend to become disillusioned with the bureaucratic, stilted management practices taken from the industrial modes of the 1920s. The TRW model is one antidote. Obviously, government agencies involved in human service areas can do more and better in terms of relating their structure to their management.

6. Response:
The Universities

A severe schizophrenia exists in the nation's higher education system regarding anything more specific than "Princeton in the nation's service." On the one hand, there are the outreach programs: state universities all over the country, Columbia's Urban Center, Temple's community training projects, the third phase of Clark Kerr's multiversity. On the other hand, there is Jacques Barzun's eloquent argument that world-changing is not the business of a university, whose mission is study and contemplation, teaching and research. This dichotomy is real. It shows in the manner in which universities have approached the crisis in public service leadership. Self-development has generally been denigrated by the university, whose bureaucrats have sought to use academic credentialism to ban career entry and development both within its own walls and beyond.

Two small, experimental incentive programs demonstrated in the 1960s how weak universities are in community development potential:

(1) The Ford Foundation poured millions of dollars into land-grant universities to test the possibility that the great rural extension of the American past could be transformed into urban extension for

the future. There were several variations, but the basic idea was to create a new urban extension agent who would bring the blessings of research and technology into the central city. By 1966, Ford concluded that the experiment had not been successful and phased out its support.

(2) In the late 1960s, the federal government allocated a lot of build-up and a pitifully small amount of money to Title I of the Higher Education Act, Community Service and Continuing Education. Funded through state education departments under state plans, Title I provided small subsidies (the larger states received a little over a quarter of a million dollars in good years) to community service initiatives of public and private colleges.

Neither of these programs had any impact for institutional change on universities. The university management usually swallowed the money by setting up appendage institutes or centers. When the outside funds stopped, the appendages could be cut off and the university was not the loser. (The analogy is to large private corporations which take on government contracts, as in the defense field, rather than to public agencies, although there is some overlap.)

Only in the last couple of years have universities begun to create new programs, with credit for work and participation combined with periods of study and analysis. VISTA and the Antioch and Northeastern work-study programs offer models of participation-credit. Many educational critics have described how tasks in hospitals, environmental agencies, social services, child care and economic ventures can be seen as part of participatory training. Such activities, synthesized during periods of intense study, can be the roots of true practical education for leadership.

Close to 100 universities offer some form of public administration program. Among these programs, however, few offer service in the three areas of major need cited by Frederick Mosher seven years ago: refresher education in fields of specialization, basic and refresher training in management and broadening and refresher education in the social and policy sciences. (Mosher in Jones, *ed.*, p. 134.)

In the 1950s, there was a great deal of concern in university circles that university programs were not turning out people to be effective public service managers.

Yale Law School was perhaps the first major professional school to make a commitment to public service in an effective way. By revising its traditional legal curriculum and placing emphasis on broader social concerns, Yale was consciously attempting to broaden career opportunities for its graduates. In reality it was also adjusting to what was happening to the successful Wall Street lawyer, continuing what had become a typical path: successful partners and even junior partners in the major firms would do four year "tours" in Washington or overseas. Despite their lack of training and dearth of managerial experience, they were the prime manpower pool for top management jobs at Defense, State and elsewhere.

The Woodrow Wilson School of Public and International Affairs at Princeton began to articulate a clear leadership preparation orientation in the early 1950s. Its emphasis then was on becoming a feeder for policy positions in the State and Defense departments. It hoped to offer a broader outlook than the more traditional schools such as Boston's Fletcher School of Law and Diplomacy. In the 1960s, the Woodrow Wilson School shifted to the younger generation's preoccupation with domestic affairs.

In its imperial phase, the University of Pittsburgh built a new graduate school of public and international affairs. Under the aggressive leadership of Dean Donald C. Stone, the school attempted to focus on areas of critical need in government. It provides both degree and nondegree programs in urban affairs, public works engineering and administration, public administration, economic and social development, and international affairs.

Pittsburgh's program in public works engineering and administration is particularly interesting and unique. Probably over $50 billion is spent in this field, which is of key importance to the nation's environment. Yet there appear to be no other university programs aimed specifically at developing the manpower to spend this money effectively.

Harvard, Johns Hopkins and a number of other major universities began to provide various types of graduate programs for young people interested in leadership roles in public service, but not in the traditional scholarly or professional degree efforts. Like Princeton, Harvard has moved on to provide professional outlets as well: it now has a Ph.D. program in public policy. Stanford provided a Public Affairs Fellowship program designed to offer "education, not training" for persons interested in public policy careers.

Support for these endeavors came in 1963, when the Ford Foundation financed a National Institute of Public Affairs (NIPA) program. Promising mid-level career executives were sent to universities for a year of academic study. While perhaps less "relevant" than NIPA's fellows program during the depression of the '30s, it did give government managers (from other than the Defense and State establishments) a year of quality graduate work.

Charismatic individuals had a great deal to do with developing the most popular of these new prestige academic centers. Max Millikan and Walt Rostow, at their MIT center (later noted for its early CIA sponsorship), drew a number of economists and political economists into public policy and management careers. William Mosher, Paul Appleby, Harlan Cleveland, and later Steven K. Bailey did the same for the state and local government scene from the Maxwell School at Syracuse University. The Maxwell School has been a significant source of public administrators at all levels. Bailey's successful initiatives in the 1960s brought it into the international field. Like the University of Michigan's public administration program, Maxwell attracts the young person who has already made a commitment to public service and may have a couple of years experience. Maxwell has also been a progenitor of good researchers in the fields of practical administration and politics.

The fact that a number of policy-oriented professors moved to Washington with the Kennedy Administration in 1961 only enhanced the reputation of their schools as feeders for government services.

Donald Herzberg has focused on the needs of state governments and particularly state legislatures in the program at the Eagleton Institute of Practical Politics at Rutgers, The State University in New Jersey. With Jesse Unruh of California helping, Herzberg has made Eagleton's specialized, low-volume M.A. program unique in its field.

Eagleton stresses citizen participation in politics and improvement in the quality of government. Its concentration on the states has led to two other important concerns: the role of women in politics and the politics of mass transportation.

New York's City University created a major innovation in the John Jay College of Criminal Justice, a school which provides policemen and others an opportunity for concentrated and useful study. The emphasis is on knowledge and credentials rather than skills, but the initiative is a significant one.

The leading business schools remained on the boundaries of these efforts. As business schools began to focus more and more on methodology and organization development, their outstanding professors felt themselves becoming more and more relevant to the concerns of large public organizations. Like the law schools, business curricula offered students a combination of expertise in fields of government management and the more exciting business opportunities such as those with large international firms—or with international agencies such as the World Bank and the International Monetary Fund.

The large state universities and major urban universities had a longer history of programs attuned to the needs of their communities. Surprisingly, however, many of these were highly academic in content and teaching form, and few offered relevant internships in the agencies towards which the students were pointed. Large universities, closer to the action, stuck to the traditional patterns and grades and then recommended students to enter positions in the civil service—when they had their degrees.

The problems of the university attempting to provide a reservoir for public service leadership talent are perhaps more imposing than the successes. The professional schools, such as Yale Law and Harvard Business, are constantly pulled by the professional forces which dominate them and are more interested in training more effective lawyers and businessmen than in filling the government management gap. Similar concern for professionalism pervades schools where economists and political scientists have had strong policy sway for many years. There has always been interdepartmental conflict at the Woodrow Wilson School over control and orientation of the program. Should the training in economics at a school of public and international affairs aim toward a staff job at the IMF or at a policy job in the State Department? For many years the former was the more valued orientation.

Professional concerns are nomally reflected in financial support. The Woodrow Wilson School is the most fortunate in achieving financial independence at one fell swoop, with a single donation of $32 million in the early sixties. The Littauer School at Harvard also had strong financing. The Fels Institute at the University of Pennsylvania, known primarily as a training ground for city managers, has good financial support for a limited program. Many other well-motivated efforts, however, foundered on the rocks of university departmental rigidity and on their lack of ability to attract outside financial endowment. Professors could not afford to teach in interdisciplinary programs outside normal departmental walls. The adventurous might have attempted it had financial support for such schools been more adequate.

A further weakness of the prestige schools was their selections policy. In this decade of student power it has become almost common for officials of public service training schools to admit that they tended to select as students those most likely to succeed in government—with or without graduate or specialized training. Recruitment of ethnic minorities by such schools as Princeton or Harvard was minimal on all fronts, not just in their public service programs. More important, however, was the almost single-minded concentration on the all-American student, already well motivated and perhaps even partially experienced. He was certain to be a success and reflect success on the school from which he came. Since students of this type expected to learn many of the specific skills required for their careers on the job, the schools could focus on the more traditional academic diet—with intellectualized high-level policy seminars perhaps the watchword for most such programs.

There are additional problems in such specialty areas of public service as educational administration. The ability of teachers' colleges and schools of education to avoid doing anything to improve the quality of educational administration, particularly in hard-pressed urban schools, has been truly remarkable. Administrative competence is still thought of as the mastery of the material in a certain number of lifeless courses, most of which have nothing to do with management or leadership. The peculiar work of people in the educational field and a true understanding of educational management problems never seems to be transmitted into the operations of educational training institutions. Such translation should be a priority for reformers in education in the future.*

The California Initiative

In 1963, under the leadership of Berkeley professor Victor Jones, a conference took place on continuing education for public administrators in state, county and city government in California. It was one of the most adequately staffed and prepared meetings of its kind.

One of the conference themes, articulated by Professor Frederick Mosher, is restated by Jones:

> It is the paradoxical, unhappy and potentially tragic fact that most of the great universities have not addressed themselves to the responsibility of continuing education of government executives in any fashion comparable to their undertakings on behalf of business administrators, lawyers, doctors, engineers, architects and a host of others in private professions. They have demonstrated less concern for the broad and vitally important education of top public administrators than for professionals in a variety of governmental specialties. . . .(Jones, p. 10.)

Mosher restated the case in the form of an extended epigram:

> Nearly four centuries ago, Francis Bacon declaimed eloquently against the educational preparation of Oxford and Cambridge for the public service.

---

*It appears that even Charles Silberman's study on *Crisis in the Classroom* (New York: Random House, 1970) pays little attention to this requirement.

The 'professory learning' of the time, he wrote, 'redounded to the prejudice of states and government with the result that. . .princes, when they would make choice of ministers fit for the affairs of state, find about them a marvelous solitude of able men; because there is no education collegiate designed to this end, where such as are framed and fitted by nature thereto, might give themselves chiefly to histories, modern languages, books and discourses of policy, so they might come more able and better finished to service of the state.' (*ibid.*,p. 132.)

The conference focused on taking time off to make the intellectual transition from specialized technical or professional routine to the "more complicated and confused world of administration and politics." It was following up a 1962 U.S. Civil Service Commission conference at Berkeley, where the Federal Executive Seminar program was discussed. A theme of the CSC conference was that the continuing education needs of federal officials were also major needs at the state and local levels. It became clear, however, that while a public administration "staff college" was needed, instruction like that at Kings Point was simply "not available in educational institutions in California."

The Stanford program was discussed, as were ongoing programs at the other major universities. Clark Kerr, then Chancellor of the University of California, described the new school of administration on the Irvine campus, designed to be "concerned with the problems of managing complex enterprises whether private or public." (*ibid.*, p. 57.)

While training in both administrative techniques and social perspectives was sorely needed, the universities could not do the job the conferees suggested needed doing.

Governor Edmund Brown stated in 1963 that California had a monumental problem of management development that was not being met: in seven years, the state would have to replace 1,000 top managers and 4,000 middle managers in the nation's second largest government. Was it done? The "training period" has elapsed. In the intervening years, California has done more than most states to strengthen its leadership development activities in the state departments, but there is little evidence that the gap has been filled.

Not long after the California Conference, the western wing of the Federal Executive Seminar opened in Berkeley. (See Chapter 8.)

Arthur Naftalin, former mayor of Minneapolis, and Mitchell Sviridoff of the Ford Foundation have described the difficulties at the local level. Naftalin sandwiches the lack of training between civil service rigidities and low salaries: rigid civil service practice discourages leadership development. Low salaries assure that developing leaders will leave municipal employment for more rewarding avenues.

Toward the '70s

At the end of the 1960s, there were still only a handful of good schools of public administration or public affairs. There were some 30 programs—some of them exceedingly narrow—in urban and regional planning. There were less than a dozen *professional* curricula in urban administration, a few on-and-off university programs for community action administrators and one public works administration program. As Dean Stone of Pittsburgh put it, "The cultural lag in modernizing University education to fulfill the needs of state and local public service is enormous." (*Hearings on Intergovernmental Personnel Act,* p. 162.)

The building of resources has been ignored for so long that, even if funds were available for training in such fields as urban development, state management, community action administration and the like, the universities could not provide relevant educational experiences.

There are federal and state dollars for support of university training activities, but they are in a few specialized fields. In 1968, 15 schools of public health received $12 million for health training. The National Institutes of Health were spending over $800 million for training and research (and that amount is being cut back now, with no reallocation to other areas). NASA was spending $136 million. By contrast, OEO was spending perhaps some $20 million, which had to be shared by university and nonuniversity training resources alike.

George Washington University's School of Education has graduate programs in employee development-human resource development, one of the few creative ties between the dormant adult education field and the new needs.

In the fall of 1970, the dean of undergraduate studies at California State College (Domiguez Hills) announced plans for an institute to develop "a new breed of future managers who would be known as urban-environmental managers."* The dean, Dr. Franklin Turner, had spent a year evaluating public management programs. As a chemist, he started with little allegiance to the public administration academic establishment. He saw his students as urban managers responsible for the quality of life through the administration of urban enviromental systems. Their training is expected to be in the social, behavioral and physical sciences, to turn out problem solvers, decision makers, policy formulators—"a new breed of professionals whose credentials include many disciplines." In addition to the new academic work involved, the program will include cooperative education work-study internships.

This type of initiative, multiplied a hundred fold, can provide the educational base for a future generation that will be better informed about the key choices to be made if Americans are to live a better life. Will it turn out leaders and managers? It is impossible to tell.

*See *New York Times,* September 21, 1970, p. 24.

7. Response: Training Outside the Universities

Across the country, a variety of uncoordinated efforts are working to meet the problem which we have defined as a weakness in leadership and managerial skills in the public service. Many are creative responses to challenges in limited areas. A great number re-invent the wheel in terms of methodology. Few know what the others are doing. All appear to have as common ground the sure knowledge that the political leaders of agencies in the public service, at all levels, prefer simple on-the-job training to all other forms of personnel development. And Frederick Herzberg's "job enrichment" may have some tough sledding in industry; but his ideas, in diluted form, are popular in government.

Many responses come in training or educational forms. As Leonard Nadler summarized these approaches, training's function is to improve performance on the job. Education helps a person move to a higher position within the organization. Nadler adds the concept of "employee development" to cover activities concerned with preparing a person to move with the organization as it develops, changes and grows. The specific behavioral objectives which validate a training program and have some applicability in an educational activity are inappropriate for the broader development programs. (Nadler, 1971.)

Training, education and development services are provided by governmental trade or professional associations, by private companies and by foundation-supported special-purpose nonprofit entities.

ICMA and the Professional Association Approach

The International City Management Association is the professional organization of municipal managers. It has a strong developmental thrust to increase the proficiency of city managers and other administrators and thereby promote professional management.

Since 1935, its Institute for Training in Municipal Administration has offered correspondence courses to over 50,000 municipal managers. These courses are "programmed" and can be run by local leaders for groups. They contain texts and manuals, study guides, tests, special cases and leaders' guides; they also provide individualized comments and grading by an instructor.

The courses cover broad areas. For example, Managing the Modern City describes the developing city, the role of the administrator, organization theory, modern management tools and a number of specific administrative functions. There is a Supervisory Methods in Municipal Administration course, as well as "Administration" programs in a number of functional areas: personnel, finance, police, fire, public works, library and public relations.

More recently, ICMA has been joining forces with other organizations to provide more complex and useful programs for municipal managers. This change in emphasis is consciously directed at the leadership and management "crisis" in government. A key one-week traveling seminar on Managing Human Resources in Public Agencies is being presented for the first time in 1970-71 by a team from the Industrial Relations Center of the University of Chicago, co-sponsored by the Public Personnel Association. The first-year phase covers management and leadership styles, understanding human behavior and dealing with group behavior within the organization and in the community setting—obviously with a broad-brush in a five-day exposure. The second year will cover effective communication and coaching and developing a staff; the third will cover problem-solving, decision-making and management by objectives.

ICMA has also contracted with Blake's Scientific Methods, Inc., for one-week introductory Managerial Grid Seminars. The seminars bring to urban management problems a "guide to meeting several critical management needs":

1. Improving personal leadership effectiveness
2. Evaluating the work culture
3. Building teamwork
4. Improving intergroup relations
5. Applying learning to achieve results
6. Planning effectively

These seminars cost participants $300-400 per week, plus transportation to a regional location, room and board. The correspondence courses are much less expensive, of course.

A number of governmental trade associations offer courses and conferences of varying duration and quality to their members. The main input is usually informational, with little direct attention to skills and attitudes.

Associated with government's training efforts are those of a host of training and consulting companies (now said to number in the thousands). They provide service to the federal agencies and to the state and local program units created to utilize federal grants. There is no particular coherence in the system: the field is a late-blooming free enterpriser's dream—chaotic, entrepreneurially oriented, creative, fast moving.

Almost everyone plays. The established giants in the consulting business—Arthur D. Little, Booz Allen, Cresap McCormick and Paget, McKinsey—may be bidding against small firms set up last year by a couple of ex-federal employees. Wolf and Company or Peat, Marwick and Livingston may be bidding against the latest all-black entry into the business. Big industrial outfits—Lear Siegler, Volt,

Westinghouse Learning, General Learning—come up against firms with strong university bases or connections such as Sterling Institute, OSTI or Project Associates. Environmetrics will offer the latest in computer-assisted urban problems games; Kepner-Tregoe offers its rational problem-solving and decision-making system. Bell and Howell's Human Development Institute will package into tapes, cards and manuals the most complex kinds of training for improved communication and human interaction. Educational Systems and Design will develop a package that meets specific departmental needs, with a focus on role-play and structured interaction.

The organization that in many respects is a "father" of this system, National Training Laboratories, despite its nationwide scope and reputation, has become another bidder on the governmental scene, putting its emphasis on sensitivity training and the T-group on the line against competitors using similar or totally different learning systems.

The new firms include many types of people. There are firms made up largely of Peace Corps veterans. There are veterans of Manpower, Head Start, Job Corps. The War on Poverty veterans sometimes divide ethnically into white, black or Latin firms. Integrated firms and "segregated" ones work together for mutual advantage. Many look like the defense contractors who employ retired military officers. The training outfits develop in this way because of mutual interest, entrepreneurial opportunism and technological expertise.

Unfortunately, governments have not learned to use these firms effectively. They are normally called in for a one-shot purpose, a survey or needs assessment or to conduct three days of training on a specific subject. The longest duration is usually 12 months of service in a generally defined area. Such short shots often fail to utilize the outside firm effectively. It is certainly difficult to dovetail such efforts into a comprehensive organization development plan. Perhaps only OEO among federal agencies has attempted to realize a more coherent job from outside consultants. (See Chapter 8.) OEO put out to bid large chunks of year-long training, with relatively clear objectives and an evaluation system.

The major talent pool which these firms offer to the government has not yet been harnessed in any meaningful way, however. In the nature of an unstructured, classically free enterprise approach to a problem, this lack of utilization may not be harmful. Much of the private sector operates the same way.

Perhaps the most sophisticated private firms engaged in the technology of executive development, however, are turning toward longer term arrangements, more permanent combinations of in-house staff and outside consultants, and more accountability and cost effectiveness. There is no special reason for government to remain 20 years behind the times.

As mentioned previously, one useful developmental strategy in industry has been the system developed and trademarked by Robert Blake and his associates, the managerial grid. Blake describes the grid organization development system as one which helps the manager understand:

1. How the organizational culture influences the ways men think and feel and their will to achieve
2. The properties and skills of "synergistic teamwork"
3. The dynamics of the behavior of others
4. The dynamics of his own behavior (Blake & Mouton, 1969, p. 59, *passim.*)

The Blake system has been put to the test in a number of different industries. Despite its rhetoric, it seems to have great appeal to the better educated manager and researcher in modern-technology-based organizations. One of its attractions is that it is a long-term, comprehensive approach which keeps the whole organization in focus. Its successful implementaion usually appears to imply a commitment with top management support of two to five years.

For this reason it may remain of limited use in the public sector. Organizations there turn over too rapidly. Executive leadership is usually measured in two-year segments of four-year terms. At the local level, two-year terms are not uncommon. The political focus of public service employment is especially critical in the newer areas of grant-in-aid programs for social purposes, the area of major concern for this study. While well-established quasi-public agencies responding to key needs recognized in past generations—the Tennessee Valley Authority, Atomic Energy Commission and Port of New York Authority come to mind immediately—have been able to undertake long-range organization development programs, more recent organizational forms have not had that luxury. Community Action Agencies at the local level are still often considered as permanent as a runaway garment sweatshop. Model Cities and Concentrated Employment agencies have gone through several "reorganizations," with more coming as organizational missions are revised. Their parents in Washington have faced problems of rapid turnover and, more recently, of a large number of vacant or "acting" executive positions.

Grid organizational development poses some challenges to the public executive of the 1970s. Like other well-articulated management improvement systems, it requires a level of leadership, a continuity of effort and a commitment of funds beyond any shown in public service in the 1960s.

SEDFRE

The Scholarship and Education Defense Fund for Racial Equality, a nonprofit educational organization, devotes much of its training capability to working with newly elected or appointed black public officials. SEDFRE has provided training and technical assistance services to black mayors and city administrations in Gary and Fayette and for black Board of Education members and elected officials nationwide.

SEDFRE director Ronnie Moore has understood the dangers of the one-shot training effort. When resources permit, he will station a skilled "change agent" in the community to provide long-term service.

SEDFRE's training often concentrates on improving communications, group building and human relations. It has provided an invaluable resource to its primary constituency. Its services have also been used by a number of school systems and community agencies.

Ford's Initiatives

From the record thus far, the Ford Foundation has clearly been the major financial resource for new approaches to leadership development in government. It is also clear that long years of Ford subsidies to universities and academically oriented policy centers did not pay off in significant leadership development or institutional change. In the 1960s, beginning with some early initiatives of Christopher Edley and others concerned with government and community operations, the foundation began to test training strategies. The tests were not part of a coherent plan. No monitoring or evaluation system was built in to assure that grants for training might be assessed so that the findings could guide future policy. The individual grants, however, funded such interesting experiments as Urban Fellows, the Manpower Assistance Project, Urban Training Center, North City Congress and Penn Center.

Urban Fellows

The Ford Foundation and the U.S. Conference of Mayors had long been interested in the development of leadership talent for municipal service. Early Ford "Great Cities Grey Areas" programs, 1962 vintage, usually made at least vague reference to development of fresh talent. Paul Ylvisaker was in charge of Ford programming at the time. He tended to prefer that local programs raid local universities, such as Yale in New Haven. He also favored informal developmental activities and internships under city officials to formal training. John Gunther and Hugh Mields of the Conference staff and Allan Talbot, who worked for Mayor Lee of New Haven, put together a number of ideas; but no program ever jelled.

When Mitchell Sviridoff became Vice President for National Affairs at Ford, he was interested in a program which would tie the need for training local government leaders to another: the scarcity of well-trained municipal leaders from minority group community organization backgrounds.

After nearly 10 years of talk and planning, Frank Logue, ex-director of New Haven's Community Action Institute, put the package together in 1969. The Urban Fellows program was designed to provide training and was done in collaboration with Yale University. The first 30 trainees served internships with such effective leaders as Mayor Alioto of San Francisco and Mayor Stokes of Cleveland. For the most part, the trainees were blacks, Puerto Ricans and Mexican-Americans who had been CAP directors, department heads or program managers in their home communities. This internship of a year in a work situation in close proximity to a savvy municipal official was designed to prepare the trainees for even more significant urban service in the future.   The interns can earn M.A. credits under an arrangement with Pepperdine College. In the 1930s, the National Institute of Public Affairs (NIPA) Fellows were expected to go on to major posts in the federal service. Many did. Success for the Urban Fellows project will probably be measured by the number of mayors it produces.

MAP

A similar Ford-financed endeavor in a more specialized area is the Manpower Assistance Project (MAP). A pioneer in contemporary internship programs, MAP is designed to develop managers of manpower programs through a combination of preparatory and on-the-job training in manpower agencies. MAP works closely with the Department of Labor. It provides free technical assistance to manpower projects. The quality of service opens doors for its trainees. It was begun by George Bennett and Thomas Flood, who each had five years of experience as manpower innovators and managers of successful projects in New Haven and Boston. MAP is currently working to make the urban community field experience acceptable for academic credit, much as are field studies in geology and internships in medicine. Bennett has proposed to Tufts University that the MAP intern program be merged into a master's program in manpower management. Tufts faculty would provide formal teaching and materials preparation. MAP staff would provide the field supervision. The internship would take seven months of a four-semester master's program. It would include experience in field operations, a continuing seminar based on field problems and field research leading to a thesis.

Bennett is also hopeful that cross-fertilization of the two staffs will make the academics more adept at working in the manpower field and will integrate practitioners into the university system. He has developed the program with a strong academic base, assuring that the argument of "lowering standards" cannot be used against it.

Similar internship activities in *political* processes have been provided by the Eagleton Institute at Rutgers for master's level work.

Urban Training Center

Ford also financed some more unusual leadership development programs which depend less on on-the-job training with established practitioners. In one, the Urban Training Center for Christian Missions in Chicago (UTC), the urban leadership result was somewhat accidental. Ford provided funds to enable selected black ministers from all over the country to attend UTC's training. That program is designed to re-orient ministers to urban problems and opportunities, spiritual and developmental. A number of ministers have left that calling and gone on to head social and economic programs in manpower, housing, minority business development and others.

UTC also utilized and popularized a training device, the "plunge," which is now used in federal and state training around the country. The plunge is an experimental training tool of great impact. A trainee dresses in old clothes. He is dropped at Skid Row, a port of entry or other urban slum neighborhood. He has only a couple of dollars in his pocket, usually no identification. His job is to stay alive and to test the public, religious and private services available to residents of the neighborhood. He usually will remain in the plunge for four or five days, perhaps with one or two group meetings to relieve his sense of isolation and to provide a forum for learning.

The plunge may be the individual's counterpart of the T-group experience. It can have significant effect on a person's attitudes and is a learning device of great power. It can bring the bureaucrat up against the reality of the service he is administering: the impersonality of the welfare interview, the coldness and inefficiency of the hospital clinic, the invisibility of the community services agency. Often, the realization of something as small as the complete lack of public toilet facilities in slum neighborhoods will cause significant reorientation and learning.

North City Congress

Ford contributed a small grant to a Philadelphia organization, the North City Congress (NCC), which has an entirely different strategy for leadership development in North Philadelphia. In a black ghetto community of some 300,000, North City Congress provides a host of supportive services to neighborhood organizations and thus frees their leaders for action. NCC offers fiduciary services for Model Cities and other programs, publishes a "community calendar" which describes everything that is going on in the area; researches position papers on major issues which affect the community, and offers relatively unstructured leadership development seminars. NCC's supportive and facilitating role and the leadership of its director, Alvin Echols, have won it firm support from all black factions and respect in the rest of the Philadelphia community.

Penn Center

The leadership development projects in this selective list have at least one thing in common: they are run by sophisticated urban generalists. Most trainees are fairly well experienced. In the rural South, however, sophisticated, progressive leadership is hard to find. Services provided by federal and state programs traditionally discriminate against black citizens, particularly where such key economic instruments as farm price supports and cooperative extension services are involved.

In 1967 Penn Community Center, a Quaker outpost in Frogmore, South Carolina, took on the job of providing leadership training services for the rural poor. It brought a series of trainee groups to Frogmore, provided them with an intensive 15-week training and living experience, and sent them back to their home communities. At one point, it provided personnel to follow them up on their return home and help them develop programs. Penn's experimental program was spread thinly and was beset by management problems in a time of rapidly evolving social attitudes in the South. It did, however, point to the significant need to build indigenous leadership in the most deprived areas of the country, without which even the most enlightened federal programming probably cannot work.

There is perhaps more concern now than at any time since the Depression for more human and humane approaches to public problems. The resources for management development are rich and varied throughout the country and the private and independent sectors can contribute a great deal.

8. Response: Government Training Initiatives

The direct federal efforts at management training have been somewhat haphazard and weak. They reflect a congressional attitude that is prevalent in most of America: hire a man qualified for the job and he should not need any training. The domestic agencies for the most part were ignoring training in the mid-1960s. The defense establishment had significant systems in place. After the Government Employees Training Act was passed in 1958, the Civil Service Commission turned its attention back to traditional personnel policy concerns, while a few of its progressive members and training staff worked to create executive development programs. In its cursory 1967 report, the House Subcommittee on Manpower and Civil Service complained:

> The Civil Service Comission has devoted most of its 60-man Washington training staff to conducting a wide variety of interagency training courses. It has done too little in (1) monitoring Federal training programs, (2) evaluating training methods, facilities and equipment, (3) reviewing and analyzing the total training effort, (4) providing the Congress with adequate information on the total training effort.

It was the Peace Corps that perhaps most effectively brought training as an issue to the attention of the federal establishment.

Peace Corps

The Peace Corps has shown a great deal of flexibility as well as a firm commitment to training since its beginnings. The focus and scope of that training has changed with Peace Corps policy shifts. In his introduction to Jules Pagano's booklet on "Education in the Peace Corps," Peter Siegle notes that "the fundamental principle of Peace Corps training is the notion of total cultural immersion. The ultimate effect is a 'liberally educated' volunteer." Through field experience and direct teaching, trainees absorb language, customs and attitudes. Then they meet natives and workers from the land to be served. Returning volunteers are also used as trainers. (Pagano, p. vii.)

The Peace Corps has had to teach technical skills, human relations, language and culture. They developed an in-house capability, hired a number of private contractors, and used a variety of colleges and universities. At this point, most training contracts are put out to bid. Nine years of experience has given Peace Corps officials a sophisticated and knowledgeable approach to judging competence.

Peace Corps training clearly was intended to seed American educational theory and practice with reform. Pagano points to significant reforms in such universities as Wisconsin, Hawaii, Western Michigan, Washington and UCLA. New courses were developed to prepare Americans to serve overseas; graduate degrees in international service were initiated; some of the first summer study and service internships in domestic social problem areas were offered. (*ibid.*, p. 10.)

A favorite Peace Corps contractor in the 1965-70 period was David Lilenthal's Development and Resources Corporation. D & R has been most active in India, Brazil and several countries in Africa. Its speciality is agriculture and rural community development. Its Peace Corps competence came out of long in-house experience in bringing Americans into difficult growth situations in developing countries.

D & R uses a comprehensive curriculum design system which approaches programmed instruction in its tightness. Its trainers have overseas experience. They stress agricultural skills and knowledge of the country. The discipline and methods learned in this kind of training are useful to volunteers when they return to the United States.

Other Peace Corps training has followed the attitudinal road. A good deal of early training for volunteers going to Latin America took place in Puerto Rico. There, the therapeutic influence of Dr. Efren Ramirez, a psychiatrist who had great success using attitudinal confrontation in dealing with narcotics addicts, was extremely strong. (Ramirez later went to New York as that city's first Commissioner of Addiction Services.) The Ramirez approach was brought into community development training through ex-Peace Corps trainers. David Borden, for example, used it in his experimental Block Communities Project in East Harlem in the mid-1960s.

Peace Corps staff itself, under Pagano and Paul Delker (both of whom later moved on to the Office of Education), undertook direct training of volunteers. They experimented with new materials and techniques. Delker introduced heavy emphasis on case studies and role play, which was designed to sensitize volunteers to complex cultural differences. These techniques have proved useful in community development training at home.

Federal Executive Seminar Centers

When John Macy was Chairman of the U.S. Civil Service Commission in the early 1960s, he was able at last to help initiate training services for career government executives. There had been studies during the Eisenhower Administration. The Committee on Economic Development was preparing its report, "Improving Executive Management in the Federal Government," issued in 1964.

In 1963, the first Federal Executive Seminar Center opened at Kings Point, New York. It was followed in 1966 by a center in Berkeley, California. A third center is in the planning stage. The two centers handle some 1,700 trainees each year, usually for two to three week management education seminars. Over 7,000 federal managers had attended by the end of 1970. Their average age is 45.

They are primarily at the GS-14 level, the next-to-highest regular Civil Service rung. (Policy-makers are civil servants at grades GS-16–GS-18, and other presidential appointees in different pay categories.) They come from 50 different governmental departments. Just under a third are from the military, the most avid user of government training services. They average 17 years of government service. About three-fourths are college graduates.

The methods used are similar to those in leading academic graduate schools, the military service colleges and the State Department's Foreign Service Institute. Prominent outsiders, chiefly academicians but often senior government officials and businessmen, lecture and lead group discussions. The reading lists are extensive. Small group assignments are buttressed by field trips. Small group involvement ranges from visits to Mobilization for Youth and the Bell Telephone training center to co-learning with a group of oceans systems specialists from Grumman.

The content spreads over a number of areas. The "core courses" and the most popular appear to be the following: Management of Organizations, Federal Program Management, Administration of Public Policy and Environment of Federal Operations. These are two-week (ten-day) courses. Other more specialized courses include: The National Economy and the Federal Executive, Social Programs and Economic Opportunities, and Administration of National Security Policy.

The Civil Service Commission Executive Seminar Center brochure points out:

> As the technical and administrative ability of career executives became more important, the need for broader understandings by careerists about total purposes and activities of government became more apparent, and the realization grew that effectiveness of Government operations depends largely on the ability of those at or near the top of the career ranks.
> The objective of the Executive Seminar Center Program is to provide courses of instruction designed to broaden the conceptual understanding and to enchance the administrative abilities of mid-level executives from all

departments and agencies at that point in their careers when attained or potential position and responsibility dictates that they expand their views, attitudes, and understandings beyond agency and functional boundaries.

Harry Wolfe, director of the Berkeley Seminar, sees the experience as an educational one, with no training intent. As opposed to the Kings Point military academy environment, the Berkeley setting obviously is more conducive to broadening the perspectives of government officials and helping them understand the relations between government and society.

Wolfe gets cooperation both from the university and the Berkeley "scene." Federal executives can go to classes in public administration, talk to students about war and public health (drugs), and use their main-drag hotel as headquarters for late-night bull sessions. They certainly learn to relate to their children's generation.

Evaluation of the Federal Executive Seminars is difficult. On the rating sheets, two-thirds of the trainees have found the seminars "excellent," and most of the rest say "very good." In correspondence with the author, William R. King, the director at Kings Point, notes:

> The evaluative data on improved performance back on-the-job is gathered by the seminar participant's individual agency. The departments and agencies participating in the program over the past six years have continually increased their requests for spaces in our programs, indicating their immense satisfaction with the effect of the seminar experience on their staff. Requests for spaces are currently running about three times greater than our facilities permit us to fulfill.

The experience undoubtedly is educationally enriching. Do the trainees bring back new knowledge, skills and attitudes which make a difference on the job? Would a similar program among executives in the same work group produce more organizational change? Would an individualized needs assessment process make for more efficient training? There are no simple answers to these questions.

One unusual facet is that the commission encourages agencies to send managers to "program-related" seminars *not* directly related to their work. There is an attempt to promote government-wide ecumenism to enlarge the background of the federal executive and thereby help prepare him to assume responsibility in a wide variety of programs. The developmental process as the Bureau of Training of CSC sees it is made up of the following stages:

1. *Supervisory Development*—develops skills required for the directing of individual effort toward the accomplishment of desired goals.

2. *Managerial Development*—develops the skills required for achieving the most effective utilization of available resources: men, material, money and facilities. Develops the understanding of organizational goals and the ability to achieve these goals through the coordination and direction of group efforts.

3. *Selective Asssignments*—provide practical experience and understanding of other organizational entities.

4. *Specialty Instruction*—reinforces on-site knowledge and minimizes time to acquire depth of understanding.

5. *University, Fellowship Instruction*—assists in the preparation of capable specialists with recognized potential to assume administrative and executive managerial positions by broadening the knowledge, concepts and perspectives of our society, government, economy and "way of life."

6. *Executive Development*—broadens the understanding and acceptance of the functions of other groups within the organization and of related government entities. Develops the conceptual understanding of government as an integral part of society and the means through which government achieves society's goals.

7. *Advanced Executive Development*—develops the conceptual understanding of process and prerequisites to the establishment of public programs and policies and the anticipation and removal of obstacles to their implementation.

Federal Executive Institute

The higher level executives have a new training center, the Federal Executive Institute (FEI) in Charlottesville, Virginia. For the some ten thousand supergrade career managers (out of the three million people in the Civil Service), the Civil Service Commissioners set up FEI in 1968 and kept control of it in their own office. They have since opened its facilities to small numbers of top-rank state and local officials.

FEI is just getting started, but it already has built a number of innovations onto the Federal Executive Seminar experience. It calls itself a "learning community," where executives, a full-time faculty of six academics and six experienced government executives, and "distinguished visitors" meet for "mutual exchange and exploration of knowledge and concepts, thus broadening managerial perspectives and gaining in-depth insight from each other on the problems and priorities of today's public service."

According to its brochure, the broad educational goals of FEI are three:

1. To heighten career executive responsiveness to national needs and goals
2. To increase their appreciation of the totality of the governmental system
3. To improve their knowledge of managerial processes

The institute expects to conduct intensive eight-week residential programs for about 300 executives each year. Their budget, like that of the Federal Executive Seminars, is made up of charges against departments and agencies for executives who attend. In 1970, the charge was about $3,250 a head, providing an annual budget of close to a million dollars.

In addition, a key element of the FEI is its close ties with the University of Virginia. A Ford Foundation grant pays for university staff and students in cooperative ventures with the institute. The federal executives use the university's library and other facilities.

The learning methodology is by far the most sophisticated among federal training programs. It includes a number of group dynamics elements as well as more traditional academic training strategies. These include:

1. Executive development groups, small clusters for orientation, learning goal-setting, resource evaluation and assessment of progress toward goals.
2. Workshops, usually intensive participatory sessions involving leadership, executive skills and national needs and goals. The executive skills workshop has focused on two areas: (a) individual skills the executive needs to perform his leadership task, and (b) rational decision-making processes imposed on the executive as decision-maker.
3. Policy-management studies, providing individual or small group options for intensive work on specific problems.
4. Seminars, differing in content but focused on the three major objectives of the institute.
5. Lectures, both by distinguished public figures brought in for an evening and by executives themselves, many of whom are the leading experts in their fields.

The FEI is a serious venture with a serious view of the government executive in a revolutionary period. Into eight weeks it attempts to cram growth in terms of *self, manager, membership in a government* which has policy and direction, and *responsibility to a broader society.* FEI's birth was difficult and controversial, as its operations continue to be. It appears that early efforts to have much less structure and a more intense personal experience were too much for traditionalists in the government and Congress to take.

James Beck, Jr., the driving force within the Civil Service Commission for the Federal Executive Seminars and early director at Kings Point, was the organizer of FEI and is deputy director at Charlottesville. Frank Sherwood, the director, came from the School of Public Administration at the University of Southern California, where he was a professor, director of the school and consultant to numerous domestic and overseas governments. FEI's ability to turn the pressures within the Civil Service Commission, the participating government departments and the Congress to the benefit of meaningful training for high-level government executives is probably tested each day.

For a number of years, the commission has talked about lower level institutes to be located in the cities where CSC has regional offices. Such centers would respond to the needs of federal agencies with quantity demands for training. No budget has been provided for these institutes. The offices themselves provide some courses in various management and skills areas. They charge a fee, as would a private firm. The courses are often open to state and local officials. The commission in Washington provides a large number of courses in many areas and publishes reports on training throughout the federal government.

State civil service agencies, aside from the California example and others cited previously, have generally been unwilling or unable to implement a developmental strategy. The New Jersey Civil Service Commission has agressive and professional leadership in its chairman, James Alloway, and its staff director, William Druz. If a public service institute is to be created at the state level anywhere, New Jersey is now a good bet.

The OEO Experience

Many of the young, so-called "social scientists"* who initiated the war on poverty and initially staffed the Office of Economic Opportunity were rich in government experience and the impatience that goes with it. They were determined not to repeat the mistakes of earlier opportunity programs. They had a relatively clear perspective on the need for thousands of newly trained managers ready to take on the critical tasks of innovation, coordination, public relations and effective project implementation which the domestic "war" required.

*From Daniel Patrick Moynihan's *Maximum Feasible Misunderstanding* and the book by the same name, published by The Free Press, 1969.

Only the Peace Corps could offer a model for building training and developmental activities into a large-scale new government program. A number of the Shriver task force staff were familiar, of course, with the Peace Corps experience. They knew they could not count on universities to carry out the whole job. Universities had their own interests and were hard to move. Neither could they depend on private contractors, whose ranks normally were too thin to support a large-scale effort even when the funding was adequate.

OEO officials, particularly Sanford Kravitz and Brendan Sexton of the Community Action Program, moved to develop a training system which would apply the best of all worlds. Each region would get one or more multipurpose "training centers" financed by OEO grants. There would be no capital funds and funding would be on a year-by-year basis. OEO officials were not ready to offend the large state landgrant colleges which have political clout in Congress and are the oases of training talent in the hinterlands. They thought that urban universities might have some good people. OEO's "institutional change" strategy could be expanded to embrace such institutions, involving them more deeply in solving problems of rural and urban poverty.

Some new centers would be created. They should be responsive to the needs of disadvantaged (particularly black and hispanic) residents of the areas they served. They should be innovative in hiring, in program concept and development, in training style. They should demonstrate what effective training can do.

At the time that first grants were made in mid-1965, New England, New York and New Jersey made up only one OEO region. Presaging the Nixon administration's sensible restructuring of that populous monstrosity into two regions, Kravitz granted funds for a New England center and a New Jersey center. As an afterthought, New England would include upstate New York; New Jersey might take in New York City. The first was to be housed with New Haven's Community Progress, Inc. (CPI), one of the most successful of the pioneer (pre-OEO) urban anti-poverty programs. The center, called the Community Action Institute, was to be an autonomous arm of CPI, governed under policies of the CPI board. CPI in turn was to provide field experience and on-the-job training for trainees coming to the Mecca of economic opportunity programs.

The other center was to be a bigger risk. With strong interest from its governor, Richard Hughes, and energetic leadership, New Jersey had initiated one of the strongest state economic opportunity offices in the country. Under its first director and deputy, John Bullitt and Joel Sterns, it had evinced a keen interest in training at all levels. New Jersey's first generation community action program directors—in Newark, Atlantic City, Trenton, Paterson and a number of county and multicounty agencies—were also strong. Among them were two of the authors of the HARYOU program in Harlem—Cyril Tyson and Kenneth Marshall. There was potential for conflict between a state-run training effort, perhaps at Rutgers, The State University, and training efforts at the community level. The Rutgers Labor Center had an OEO grant for a community action intern program, designed to provide training and work experience in the new community action agencies for uncredentialed veterans of civil rights and trade union struggles.

Brendan Sexton, the United Automobile Workers' education director, was at OEO in charge of the training grants. Sexton arranged a compromise structure. A broad-based 21-man board would be created. The governor and the president of the State University each would appoint one permanent member. Seven CAP directors would serve. The other twelve seats would have the controlling interest. They included: seven representatives of poverty target areas around the state and five representatives of major interest groups (civil rights, business, labor, etc.).*

On the West Coast, OEO financed the Western Center, a separate entity tied to the extension division of UCLA. The center was to

*Initiation of the New Jersey and New Haven centers left New York City somewhat uncovered. A special organization—the New York Training Institute —was born in controversy and lived in controversy. Creation of these three centers did not prevent OEO from making some 15 single-purpose training grants in the region between 1965 and 1968. Edward Wilms, another UAW veteran, was given the task of rationalizing the system at Washington OEO.

serve seven states. It had firm support from Governor Edmund Brown. When he was replaced as governor by Ronald Reagan in 1967, the center was disbanded. In its place, OEO financed the Western Community Action Training Institute. Based on the New Jersey model with a broad-based board, WCATI still covered a multistate region until it, too, was reorganized out of existence in 1970.

So-called multipurpose centers were also created at a number of universities: Missouri, Atlanta, Oklahoma, Temple, North Carolina and Wisconsin. Only the Missouri center survived as a field training vehicle after OEO's several reorganizations of 1967-69.

OEO's management quickly became dissatisfied with the work of many of the centers. They tended to fiddle with the structures. In the region where Temple and North Carolina were working, the training job was fractioned into 18 segments; each was written into a bid document; and a number of private contractors, universities, and nonprofit organizations won contracts to perform pieces of the job.

In 1968, OEO made a small grant to the New Jersey Institute (CATI) to provide train-the-trainer services to all OEO training grantees across the country and to develop materials for use in that effort. The project was managed by Albert Fleming and utilized both CATI staff and outside consultants. This attempt at upgrading quality and developing standards was noteworthy in the history of the federal system. It lasted less than two years.

In 1969, Greenleigh Associates studied training and technical assistance for OEO. Their report concluded that OEO needed to define training more precisely and to state training goals and objectives more adequately, "particularly if training effectiveness is to be assessed." They called for more systematic recording, monitoring and record-keeping and more skills training.

Generally, OEO's training system has been characterized by a willingness to experiment and innovate and to cut losses, a concern for trainee participation, opportunities for minority group members to develop professional training expertise, and a concern for results in terms of organization-building and community organization. Only in late 1970 did it appear that the agency's experimental posture had changed and that staff development activities would be phased out, along with many of the OEO programs.

A Specific Example: The Community Action Training Institute

The New Jersey Community Action Training Institute (CATI) was one of the first organizations to attempt to draw together the strands of the various revolutions of the 1960s and to provide some form of leadership training for all the components. The strategy was not a conscious one from the start. The initial focus was on black leadership. It turned out that many of the early trainees were women with strong opinions about male-female relationships in the community action field. Young people, both black and white, were drawn to community action work. Their work backgrounds were often sketchy, particularly in terms of actual community experience. The institute had to face up early to a significant lack of politically oriented leadership in the Puerto Rican and other Spanish-speaking communities. This reality meant special programs of leadership training aimed at special, nonblack ethnic audiences.

The chairmen of the CATI board during the 1966-1970 period were two black community leaders with long trade union backgrounds, Henry Kennedy of Newark and Kenneth Peterson of the rural community of Warren Glen. They encouraged a concentration on negotiating and bargaining skills. They also assured that the trainers hired would be from or would relate well to the groups to be trained. They encouraged the institute staff to focus on capability, not credentials.

Almost all the early institute trainees had little in the way of formal educational background beyond high school. Most were entering into supervisory, management or executive positions from lower level human services jobs in traditional and highly structured agencies. They were moving into the world of public "temporary systems" for which their work backgrounds had not prepared them.

The institute developed a structured method for dealing with the training needs of individuals and organizations involved in the war on poverty. The method is oriented toward skills and behavioral change but neglects neither informational inputs nor attitudinal change. Gregory Simms, former deputy director at CATI and a veteran of both Peace Corps and HARYOU-ACT training, was the prime force in the development of the system.

The institute had to deal from the beginning with the strong ideological orientation of the early community action program. It attempted to stick to a program of teaching skills and letting each individual or organization provide its own ideological set. In an era of rapidly accelerating ethnic militance and community organization, it was difficult to deal with any problem, no matter how simple, without dealing with Black Power, political discrimination, potentials for ghetto self-determination and the like. A constant attempt was made to keep these questions as subjects of training rather than preconditions or givens.

In addition, CATI adopted a rather conscious if unschooled educational theoretical approach which rejects pedagogy in favor of Kenneth Benne's (clumsy) term, "anthropogogy." Authority relations are left relatively open to rational and situational determination. All adults are involved in processes of mutual renewal, learning, re-education. In this approach, the trainer becomes a co-learner, change agent and guide through a process whose relevance and authenticity are maintained by the training group. Yet the heart of the training method is the "clear-cut, well-defined plan for the delivery of training," as was clear from the CATI training definition at one point in its growth: "Training is any pre-planned learning experience which uses the Experiencing, Identifying, Analyzing, Generalizing (EIAG) framework to help people learn."

In turn, the key part of the planning process is the involvement and participation of the trainees. A careful *needs assessment* process means that trainees at any level are interviewed, individually and in groups. Their individual job responsibilities and functions are discussed, their work group and supervisory relations probed. They and their managers are asked about areas of needed skills improvement or development. Specific problem areas, particularly of a group process or policy nature, are elicited through survey forms and interviews.

The training team then develops a statement of needs and zeroes in on those which might be dealt with most profitably in training. That statement is checked back with the agency executives and the trainees and reviewed. When a satisfactory agreement is reached on needs, the trainers proceed to the second major task: development of a curriculum to meet the needs.

The purpose of the *training curriculum* is to lay out clearly, in narrative form, the specific objectives of the program and the methods by which those objectives will be met. The curriculum includes a schedule of training, background information on the training group and the organization, training techniques to be employed, session outlines and evaluation methodology.

The curriculum serves three critical functions: (1) it is presented to the trainees at the beginning of the program as yet another checkpoint for determining the feasibility and appropriateness of the training design, (2) it provides a road map for trainers and consultants and insures some uniformity of approach, and (3) it serves as the key reference point in the program evaluation. It is not a straitjacket, but it does provide structure and mileposts in the learning process.

The *training delivery* is geared to adult learning through contemporary participatory learning devices. Over a five-year period, CATI has emphasized certain techniques: role play and situation simulation (including video tape), laboratory exercises, case studies, discussion stimulators, programmed and other manuals, some specially made films and some supervised field work. The institute has done less with games, audio tape packages, research assignments and unstructured T-grouping.

The delivery is handled by a training team which includes both senior and junior trainers (so-called "professionals" and "nonprofessionals") and utilizes outside specialists. The internal Media Systems Division has produced special materials for use in specific programs, as well as a wide range of manuals, brochures, films, videotapes and tapes for general training use.

The critical fourth aspect of the skeletal training process described here is *evaluation*. Evaluation begins with the planning phase and ties into follow-up, as part of a closed loop or circular system. Designs often include before and after instruments which measure learning, behavioral and (sometimes) attitudinal change. Trainees also rate the content and overall effectiveness of the program and the performance of the trainers. The evaluation report describes which objectives were met, which were not, and recommends further training or other actions required to meet present objectives or new ones which evolve out of the training process.

This methodology is eclectic in the extreme. Its focus is on *practical results*.

The Institute's programs generally are oriented specifically to organization development as opposed to individual enhancement and advancement. One exception serves to illustrate the process.

CATI invited each community action agency in New Jersey and Delaware to send one "middle manager," that is, a program manager, project head, or staff person in the $7,000-10,000 salary range, to join an intensive year-long training experiment. The goals included improved functioning in several supervisory, managerial and entre-preneurial areas, aimed at raising their on-the-job productivity. They also explicitly included career advancement and mobility goals, with their organizations' directors understanding that they might become mobile beyond the confines of their agency.

The some 15 trainees were consulted and tested. They worked as a group in helping to develop a curriculum that would stress the goals in terms of knowledge, skills and attitudes they needed to advance. They wanted work in areas from "urban problems" socio-logy to team-building for the training group. The committed them-selves to eight hours a week for a year (and got agency approval to share the time).

The implementation of the program was not smooth, due to staff turnover and other problems at CATI. Yet the results were striking, even more so in mobility than in on-the-job performance. A significant number of the trainees went on to more responsible and higher paid positions either during the year or soon after. A number of the new positions were "white world" jobs as opposed to those in the anti-poverty system reserved for minority groups.

The more typical CATI program has been an effort directed at skills training for staff and board of one community action agency. A comprehensive needs assessment usually identifies a couple of areas of primary concern. Short-term programs are then initiated.

CATI will begin at any level and try to make the training quality provide the impetus for a regularized staff and board development program.

The CATI system—its eclectic methodology, the community-based policy board, the use of "nonprofessional" trainers with strong ties to the communities being served—offers one model for the development of institutions and the delivery of services to meet government's human resource development needs in the 1970s.

9. Empty Credentials and New Careers

One note must be sounded clearly in a book on leadership development: today's stress on formal academic credentials for career development, carried to its tautological extreme in New York City but an infection everywhere, is not part of the solution. Outside the State Department and the military, academic background appears to have little or no discernible relationship to job demands.* The skills of the generalist policy-maker are picked up as likely in a union hall, a large factory, or a newspaper beat as at Mory's. Unfortunately for the young, the women, and some elements of ethnic revolution, they are not picked up quite so easily in the streets. But the contemporary revolutionaries undeniably score when they point to arbitrarily high formal entrance requirements for routine jobs. Skills are skills, and schools are schools. (People need more and more education as *people* and as citizens, not necessarily to do a successful job in public employment.)

In the human services areas, the self-serving emphasis upon professionalism has helped create critical and needless manpower shortages. The "new careers" movement, spearheaded by such activists as Arthur Pearl, Frank Riessman and Russell Nixon, was

---

*Ivar Berg of Columbia University has researched a corner of this area. See his recent study, *Education and Jobs: The Great Training Robbery*, Praeger, 1970.

concentrated at first at the entry level. The concept—job first, training built in; climb the lattice through experience, training and outside education—fits as a leadership development mode as well.

In conversation and in newsletters of the new careers movement, Alan Gartner has pointed out that as a program for social change "new careers" is at the first level of development, that of a method of operation or technology. It needs a plan of implementation (or strategy) and a motor force (or constituency) if it is to succeed. Despite the mechanistic imagery, this concept offers a valuable insight into the developmental possibilities of new careers. The few government agencies interested in economic opportunities for the poor who have tried new careers programming appear to be fairly comfortable. They have done little with the other option in the theory: freeing up professionals to be more "professional," or transferring power and changing institutions with the help of new careerists.

If a government agency at any level is interested in fulfilling its commitment to equal employment opportunity for any minority— blacks, Latins, ethnics, women, young people—it need only turn to a new careers model for executive development. Such a model offers painful growth for agency and individual, but it also offers fulfillment of what up to now have been empty promises.

The new careers model encompasses job enrichment of the most progressive variety. It sees public organizations as dynamic, changing. The responsibility for development of new leadership is a key responsibility of management. As Glenn Parker defines it, the model:

> . . .requires that the jobs in a human service agency be redefined and restructured so that the unskilled workers may perform the less complicated tasks immediately on being hired; that the new workers be given time off from their jobs for training and education specially geared to their needs; that the professional staff members share some of their power, prestige and knowledge with the new workers; that interpersonal problems that may arise between the incumbent workers and the new personnel be resolved to the advantage of both; that all learn to work with each other as well-

integrated teams; that non-traditional routes to career advancement and education be charted so that the disadvantaged workers may move rapidly to positions of greater responsibility without displacing incumbent employees; that special supportive services and training in human relations for all workers be available. (Passett and Parker, p. 5.)

Because manpower shortages in health and education had to be filled in the mid-'60s, a large number of so-called "new careerists" were hired. Job restructuring proceeded, so that late in 1970 California approved the licensing of "assistant physicians." This new job title could be filled by military medics, without extensive formal pre-service education. Yet new careers programs, as described above, never came into being.

The Nixon administration changed the name of the original legislation (whose parent was Congressman James Scheuer of New York) to the Public Service Careers program. PSC changed orientation somewhat in 1970, as the emphasis moved to job development as opposed to training and upgrading. The new Labor program was designed to make it easier for the disadvantaged to reach the *first* rung of the Civil Service ladder. Senator Gaylord Nelson of Wisconsin made the PSC concept a major part of the Senate-developed manpower legislation for 1970. This legislation was designed to bring about government sponsorship of large-scale public employment in needed human services areas, a strategy associated with the Labor Department during the early Johnson administration. The budget for the major new initiative in PSC was sizeable at a time when the administration was in a budget-reducing and inflation-fighting posture. Also, PSC was considered to be tied to the Administration's major welfare reform legislation. Both measures were unresolved in the Congress at recess time in the winter of 1970.

It should be clear that the new careers mode provides an entirely new role for government executives. It forces them to focus their agency's attention and their own skills on job enrichment and training for their staff. It makes a government office a major human resource development vehicle, a far cry from the attitude which says, "Hire the best man—then tell him what to do." It takes the TRW

Systems experience and applies it to people with less educational preparation and work experience, therefore providing an even greater challenge to management. No wonder public service managers—from the Secretary of Labor to the Superintendent of Schools in Newark—have not chosen to go ahead with proposed new careers programs in their own bailiwicks.

Training and staff development areas themselves are the best places to experiment with new careers programs. People can be pulled "off the line," given training as trainers and be able (more successfully often than the personnel man or professional outside trainer) to deliver the services their colleagues need.

10. The Training Argument

A number of practitioners in the organization development field—among them Warren Bennis, Leland Bradford and Gordon Lippitt—have pointed the way to new training initiatives for more effective public programs. Senator Muskie, former Mayors Richard C. Lee and Arthur Naftalin, former Governor Terry Sanford and a number of other political practitioners have called for similar initiatives from their frames of reference. Governor Ronald Reagan has supported California's significant management development from a different perspective.

To summarize the arguments and move toward a program for action, it will first be necessary to go back a step and discuss in more detail what has been happening to government.

As organizations grow and become more complex, they require new structures and processes. New organizational forms, like the matrix management systems in the space program, become useful. Bennis' "temporary systems" approach can provide policy-makers with alternative visions to those of heavy-handed, permanent bureaucratic structures.

New forms are developing constantly. Departments of transportation at all levels are replacing (or being superimposed upon) the old roads, rapid transit and airport agencies. The thought of planning, managing and evaluating *transportation* systems is new for leaders. Similarly, "environmental protection," once a euphemism for public health, has now become a governmental organizing principle. New agencies with environmental responsibilities have such a breadth and scope that they may well provide the fertile breeding ground for a generation of generalist-administrators and political leaders.*

Where does a training program enter this process?** *First*, people have to understand a matrix system before they can apply it. There are necessary knowledge inputs. While administrators of new programs are struggling with day-to-day political realities, they must also analyze organizational needs and resources. This analytical function will require not only training but perhaps also outside consulting help. As managers attempt to adjust to a less structured mode, communications links become critical. The formal, institutionalized mechanisms are likely to be weak. Here, human relations training, with specific goals in terms of efficiency of communications, becomes a practical aid.

Second, the experience of the last decade shows that technological or policy change can make government managers obsolete. Many foreign aid program officials could not cope with the changes induced by program planning and budgeting systems which were imposed during the early 1960s. The systems analysis changes in the Defense Department promised to leave a whole generation of military officers behind.

When technology dictates more complex skill preparation, education and training, the responsibility of a staff development

* Hugh Mields, an active participant in the legislative process for most key environmental legislation of the past dozen years, had been the leader in preparing local officials to meet the new environmental challenges. He and Ron Linton have provided a framework for developing training programs in this area.

**Much of this analysis was provoked by and is based on a brilliant presentation by Leland Bradford and Gordon Lippitt at the 1969 Annual Conference of the American Society for Training and Development, Miami, May 15, 1969.

system increases. Trainers can help top managers decide on the proper mix between *individual* development (how many go to the Federal Executive Institute or the Woodrow Wilson School) and *organization development* (how much time is given to permit outside consultants to work with the management teams). The managers will be pressing for innovation and efficiency in developing people to meet program needs, and for creativity and new methods in training for complex skills. They will have to deploy technologically sophisticated people within their ranks to do some of the training, even if it means providing them with crash "train-the-trainers" exposure. These people are most likely to be up to date on the systems, software and hardware necessary for effective forward movement. Perhaps the most important thrust here, though, is training from the top in *change initiation*, so that the government agency is not always simply reacting to new technology but is moving ahead of it. The Congress has exhibited a desire to move ahead of technology recently in the air pollution field just as the executive branch did on the moon shot.

Perhaps concomitant with the opportunity of technological change is that of the accelerating "knowledge explosion." While there is general agreement at this point that an executive's education never ends, that his degrees are simply early steps in a continuing education process, little has been done to integrate work performance objectives and learning objectives. There is a clear gap between most academic programs for government executives and their growth objectives in a particular job. Most government agencies, particularly at the state and local levels, simply do not yet know how to reward growth. In addition, the host of new learning resources—from computerized data-gathering to programmed instruction—are not effectively utilized.

Trainers can most usefully assist in managing the knowledge explosion by helping people learn how to learn. Once a pattern of identification, analysis and generalization is internalized through simulated practice, an executive can cope much more effectively with a barrage of seemingly disconnected data. If he learns in addition how to manage learning resources, he will be even that much more able to cope with the barrage.

It should be noted that the revolution in modes of learning (most refreshingly identified by Marshall McLuhan) has not captured the current generation of government managers. They still get much of their information from the print medium. Since reading speeds are generally assumed to be slow, the efficiency of utilization is low. Tape cartridges, videotape and television, and staff briefings used for knowledge rather than operational matters are intruding, but slowly. The trainer can help the executive manage these new resources.

Third, as large organizations grow more complex and controlling, their staff members want more of a piece of the action. Participation is a keyword. Government managers who play with boxes on charts while social change passes them by will lose their most creative people. The agency must keep its relevance to society and must satisfy the sometimes paradoxical claims for participation on the part of its staff. The paradox comes because the loyalty of top professionals is now split between the organization and the profession. A doctor taking over at National Institute of Health splits his fealty between the Secretary of HEW and his peers in the medical profession.

The trainer can do a great deal to help government executives use the participatory paradoxes to get more effective output—if they focus themselves and the managers in an organization on an organic growth and development model, if they involve people in the setting of agency targets or objectives, and if they show executives how to use systems (job enrichment, for example) which release human energies. This current participatory thrust can be the most effective way to get at Robert Wood's concern about competence and coherence in government service.

A *fourth* potential contribution of training is in the area of confrontation, conflict and feedback—handling the new openness of disagreement in what might become a "win-win" process. Some of the new black executives hired in the war on poverty programs brought direct personal conflict into day to day government operations. Young people have followed, breaking the gentlemanly codes of repressed interpersonal behavior. Women are doing the same, although more gingerly. The amazing thing is that direct confrontation has not been greater.

This kind of feedback can lead to more efficient (and certainly more exciting) public agency behavior. What is needed is the development of programs on how to fight creatively, how to prevent a pattern of win-lose battles, and how to assure that reward systems do not coalesce around modes of interpersonal behavior rather than overall performance. Training can be a useful tool in this endeavor, particularly in showing executives how to use direct feedback to fuel the creative processes within an agency. There is some danger here that training can dip into therapy (as sensitivity training often tends to do).

The *fifth* area involves the growing importance of organizational interfaces within the government and between government and the educational and industrial systems. Our earlier discussions of the importance of personnel transferability, the dual loyalty question and the confusions of jurisdictions are pertinent here. The need for constant negotiating to get agreement for action increases as people see the interconnectedness of social and environmental problems. The Environmental Quality Act and the Intergovernmental Cooperation Act require coordinated activity in the 1970s at all levels of government beyond any heretofore practiced.*

Trainers tend to move among systems. Many have academic backgrounds and orientation, make their money from industrial clients, and want to join the great public adventures of our times. Their mobility among systems gives them good experience for helping public managers with sensing, negotiating and problem-solving skills.

The *sixth* useful role for trainers is the obvious one in an age of expanded participation and revolutionary concern, that of upgrading now under-utilized manpower. The minorities, the youth, the women, the government worker whose only escape from boredom is through union activity—all provide a severe challenge to training will

*Senator Abraham A. Ribicoff, Hugh Mields (former associate director of the U.S. Conference of Mayors) and other active proponents of this progressive legislation have warned of the management pitfalls in numerous public statements.

and technology. The trainer must help make public organizations relevant to these minorities, and help build work concepts, motivation and skills in new public servants to meet significant community and environmental needs.

All six of these areas of involvement stretch the limits of numbers and competence of the training and development practitioner.

The Requirements

The public sector needs a training and human development commitment equal to its needs. Seymour Wolfbein saw the need for such a commitment from the innards of government during a 30-year career there. When he left federal service he wrote a book on "ten commandments" for training, *Education and Training for Full Employment.* He stressed with almost pathetic urgency the need for adult education and training across the board. Paul Wishert, Board Chairman of Honeywell, estimates that U.S. corporations need 200,000 potential managers and complains that not enough is being done to fill the need. Government and the rest of the public and nonprofit sectors certainly have an equivalent requirement. (See Lindsay, p. 1,220.)

Both business and government are paying premiums for college-educated people. In most cases, that investment is under-capitalized when organizations do not follow up by investing in training on the job to meet job needs.

It is ironic that the drift in government is toward adoption of training and development systems which industry is leaving. Industry is moving away from individual improvement and moving into organization development. While schooling outside the work group has proved useful, it enhances mobility and provides "excess" skills, those which are generally useful but not needed on the job.

If a system of training and development is to be effective in improving the output of a public agency, it must focus on improving the performance of the work group as well as on the performance of the individual.

One myth which the public sector should have been able to exorcise more effectively than the private sector is that faulty individuals (rather than malfunctioning systems) are the locus of organizational problems. Bennis points out succinctly:

> For at least two decades. . .Research has shown that productivity can be modified by group norms, that training effects fade out and deteriorate if the training effects are not compatible with the goals of the social system, that group cohesiveness is a powerful motivator, that intergroup conflict is a major problem facing organizations, that individuals take many of their cues and derive a good deal of their satisfaction from their primary work group, that identification with the small work group turns out to be the only stable predictor of productivity, and so on. (Bennis and Slater, p. 115.)

Clearly, the "work group" in public programs is constantly being redefined. The anti-poverty program's nonprofit corporations broke the civil service system syndrome for implementation of many public activities. (The extensive defense and space contracting activities in the profit sector provided the model.) Large, complex tasks imply new processes and structures; the public sector has had to respond with temporary systems and new forms of organization.

As public organizations have developed interfaces with the industrial and educational world, people's careers have followed. Just as problem solving and other techniques do, leadership talent moves across the systems. So long as the flow moves back and forth, it can be looked upon as healthy cross-training. But sometimes it can become a brain drain from the public into the industrial sectors.

In discussing the problem of professional personnel for New York in 1963, D. T. Stanley hit the keynote: top management, which bears the responsibility for carrying on public programs, must assume the training responsibility, "the burden of developing an adequate supply of manpower at all levels with sufficient skills to fill necessary jobs." (Stanley, p. 288.)

Tools for the Strategy

What kind of tools does top management have at its call if its aim is to develop more effective leadership and managerial talent?

How can a systems approach to human resource development be implemented? It is important at this point to recall the adult learning theory which pervades this book.

Training can deal with improving skills, providing new knowledge, or changing attitudes and relationships. Human development in a public agency implies change and growth in individuals, work groups, and the agency itself in relation to the needs and goals of the public, as defined in legislation. A development program will help individuals upgrade their knowledge and skills, help work groups function more effectively and efficiently, help build bridges among work groups, and help the total organization to change and develop.

Leadership development tools are useful if they give the public organization manager an opportunity to:

1. *experience*: meaningful, job-related, here and now situations
2. *identify*: looking at the experience to learn what has gone on, what the people have been doing, thinking, feeling
3. *analyze*: figuring out what causes what, why the things identified are happening
4. *generalize:* applying learning from the analysis to other similar conditions

The first requisite of a leadership development activity is a clear statement of goals and objectives. Not all educational activities are useful by definition. Training tools cannot cover too much ground, and training itself is usually a slow process. The tools are only as good as the specific goals to which they are applied. Training is often mis-used as a substitute for firing, transferring, promoting or otherwise changing a situation.

Perhaps a brief discussion of some of the normal training-oriented tools will help describe where they are useful and where other strategies should be employed. Many of these modes overlap, and while their boundaries and definitions may be somewhat unclear, each has a place in the executive's arsenal. Useful tools include orientation, skills training, classroom training, on-the-job or apprenticeship training, human relations training and outside education. Useful tools not described here include job enrichment, participation in policy development, evaluation as a training device and learning through training or consultation.

Orientation

When a person takes a job in a public agency, he must acquire a new self-image, new involvements, new values, new accomplishments. (Caplow, p. 172.)

Traditionally, orientation is conducted informally in the work group. The difficulty in making formal orientation come alive is the imprecision of agency goals and the difficulty of relating imprecise goals to the specific task of a manager. Trainers or even top managers may not understand the goals—or they may want to change the goals. The orientation program may show strains if these conflicts proceed unresolved. A common example is the welfare department whose primary formal goal is determining eligibility but whose director acting as trainer in orientation stresses delivery of service as the chief goal.

An effective formal orientation program gives the new manager a chance to participate and question the material being presented and continues through his first months on the job. Breakfast or lunchtime sessions can provide time for this function without cutting into his work day.

Skills Training

A key roadblock in the path of more and more effective leadership development on the public side has been the definitional gap concerning skills training. A congressman can understand that the Air Force needs $200,000 to teach a pilot-trainee flying skills. The same congressman might ridicule the investment of $5,000 to help a new deputy assistant secretary in the new Transportation Department learn program planning and negotiating skills. Even the Civil Service Commission would appear to have blinders when it comes to developing the skills truly demanded of today's government executive. Given the federal gap, it is no wonder that state and local jurisdictions are so far behind.

The basis of skills training is helping people learn to perform their jobs more effectively—to clarify what they want to do in their jobs, to understand what their jobs demand of them, and to increase their awareness of how they work. Sometimes skills training is provided for individuals. Other times it is provided for teams or groups of people with common goals or responsibilities.

There is an obvious overlap between skills and human relations training, once again, where the government executive's crucial skills are those involved in dealing with other people.

Programmed Instruction

The programmed package can be a most effective counterpart to skills training, on-the-job training and classroom devices. The military has long exploited the strengths of the programmed instruction system: small elements of learning, conditioned reflex, positive and immediate reinforcement.

There has been little use of programmed instruction in public leadership activities, perhaps because adequate programs have not been written for complex human relations and political skills and perhaps because of an executive bias against the conditioned response.

More and more sophisticated tools appear in this field each year, however. A manager can learn PERT or any of a number of basic management skills through print packages. New technology in audio and video tapes and tape cassettes provides opportunities for teaching the full range of managerial skills. Films can be part of programmed packages. The tape provides better opportunities for feedback and individualization. Automobile tape players make it possible for executives to learn while they commute.

The great attraction to government of these packages is their relatively low cost per person. However, there is a danger that they can be overused. Some states, for example, consider a library of the best current programs to be their entire management development effort.

Generally, however, the new programmed instructional aides can be of great help in a program of management development.

Apprenticeship

The supervisor-as-trainer in an apprenticeship model is perhaps the most common pattern in public agencies, even at the highest levels. The New Haven system leaned heavily on this model.

Here, the "experiencing" is most immediate, first hand. The supervisor is usually accessible. Opportunities for identifying, analyzing and generalizing are strong. Apprenticeship should move to preceptorship, where learning and teaching are accomplished by direct observation and participation and the teacher conceptualizes the process so that the student may do more than imitate.

A key difficulty in on-the-job training in public agencies is the "sink or swim" syndrome. Traditionally understaffed, the average public manager does not have the time to conduct an orderly developmental program. He often knows little about learning theory and holds to the "watch me" school. He does not set objectives and carefully evaluate progress.

An even more troublesome problem is that of the supervisor's responsibility for evaluating employee performance. It is hard to concentrate on learning when the career risks are high. More likely to result is conforming behavior at any cost.

Coaching is an important subclassification. Formal coaching— letting a manager know what is expected of him and how he is doing, providing help when it is needed—can be the most significant of motivators. And motivation is the key to learning and growth.

Classroom Training

In discussions of contemporary training, short shrift is often given to getting the maximum use out of more traditional methods. Few public training programs at today's stage of development ignore the classroom. *Lectures* remain popular, even though the lecturers themselves know that listeners retain only a small fraction of what they hear. The importance lies in what Carl Schorske calls the demonstration of "man thinking." A public manager who hears Frederick O'R. Hayes, former federal official and New York City Budget Director, ruminate aloud about the multitude of factors—political, financial, personal, sociological—which go into a major policy decision has learned something significant. He carries away a sense of process and of the human weighing devices which operate at high levels of government. No more "scientific" breakdown of the elements to be learned can be more useful than the old fashioned lecture or dialogue for this type of learning.

Another classroom mode is the *case study*. Cases from real life or fictionalized statements of real problems are given to a group of public executives for resolution. The case study clearly discourages the grade-school attitude that there is one "correct" answer to a public policy or operational problem. It encourages group inter-action and careful analysis of factors and perceptions. The thinking remains practical: deadlines, political and managerial constraints, costs and the like are identified and dealt with.

Yet another classroom technique is *role playing*. Originally developed for therapeutic purposes and now also used in human relations training, simple role playing can be a good experiential learning device for public officials. Interdepartmental or inter-governmental problems can be explored effectively through role playing.

Games have come to our classrooms from the military, where they involved learners in interesting and enjoyable simulations of real-life situations. The immediate feedback and competitiveness of game learning schemes are attractive to managers. Computer-assisted games can compress real-world time frames and permit managers to deal with the consequences of decisions made on their piece of the world.

The problem with games, as William F. Cone of Hughes Aircraft has pointed out, is that they must operate "as though the world of management is a rational world." They are relatively simple-minded. Public managers never have all the facts; the circumstances that surround the decision-making process are seldom "rational" in the game sense. And the manager's decision is usually the beginning of the process, not the end. (Cone, p. 28)

Human Relations Training

The line between role playing and the next step in the direction of the experiential, so-called "sensitivity" training, can be thin. The name "sensitivity training" is most accurately applied to one form of human relations training, associated with the National Training Laboratories, which uses an unstructured T-group experience as the basis for learning and change. It is designed to increase interpersonal competence through an awareness of one's own motivation and the understanding of the impact one's behavior can have on others. The T-group is supposed to provide a safe environment for testing new behavior. It therefore is most properly made up of persons who do not work together day to day.

The T-group usually consists of up to a dozen people and a trainer. The group is unstructured. There is neither agenda nor set procedure. What happens depends on the needs and expectations of the participants. There is, however, a common thread that runs through most T-groups about which generalizations can be made. The first stage is the unfreezing stage. Here the members grope for a way to interact with each other. The trainer provides little or no guidance. In the process of groping a group cultural climate with a distinctive set of norms begins to evolve. The second stage is then characterized by the formation of new norms. These norms include openness, confrontation with oneself and others, "here and now" orientation, and the giving of constructive rather than evaluative feedback. These norms are designed to provide a psychologically safe environment and to encourage authentic interaction. Put simply, a person in a T-group is supposed to "tune-in" to his own feelings and behavior and "talk-up" about what he perceives and feels.

The T-group is designed to put the individual in touch with his feelings. This increased self-awareness and the psychological safety of the group allows the person to try out new behavior. In the final stage there is a stabilization of the changes in norms. Important insights into influence patterns, norms, roles, communication distortion and relating with authority are brought up again. The groups usually end by reinforcing successful changes.

There has been much political conflict about sensitivity training as a system. The Daughters of the American Revolution and the John Birch Society, among others, have labeled it a foreign, anti-American weapon, have passed resolutions condemning it, and have worked at local levels to punish public officials (particularly those in school systems) who promote or attend sensitivity sessions.

More importantly, research in the field has been somewhat vague about behavioral improvements on the job as a result of simple sensitivity training. Sensitivity trainers sometimes forget that they are supposed to be providing group management development services, not therapy. Some T-group veterans focus in on themselves and their own feelings and forget the work group.

There is little question that the T-group experience tends to provide a milieu in which individual and intragroup problems are primary. While such a focus can be useful in government or community agencies, it often takes priority over equally pressing problems or determinants: inadequate legislation or funding, opposing political forces, poor service systems and the like.*

While extensive unstructured T-groups may not have much utility in building leadership, the pragmatic use of human relations training techniques is a vital element in any development program. Learning how to listen, how to give constructive feedback, how to deal with communications problems, how to keep job tensions from building up, how feelings influence behavior, how situations influence feelings, how human relations skills are learned and built, how the micro-culture of an organization builds its own norms—all are critical to a government executive in his role as negotiator, mediator and program salesman.

*Robert Schrank has been a most persuasive analyst of the T-group process. (See Passett, 1970, Unit V, Tapes 10-12.)

A careful planning and curriculum building process can usually assure that an appropriate mix between the less structured human relations and more structured skills approaches results.

Off-the-Job-Education

There are major differences in the types of academic leave within the government service. At the federal level, the military officer has a rich choice: the war colleges, the prestige public affairs schools, or even more esoteric educational development for a fuller life. The local official, on the other hand, has had almost no opportunities beyond a night course at the local university extension service or programmed instruction from the International City Managers Association. Title VIII of the Housing Act of 1964 and Title IX of the Model Cities legislation have provided a number of free courses for the locals, but they are generally highly specialized technical offerings, taught in the traditional college manner, without college credit.

The mid-career fellowship system at the federal level has been a subject of great dispute, even though the numbers having taken advantage of the paid sabbatical are relatively few. Graduate work is supposed to be job related study which does not lead to a degree. The system provides an excellent opportunity for a highly specialized executive to undertake to broaden his skills and therefore qualify for a more significant public service role. A generalist may go back to catch up on such new specialties of the past decade as computer applications, manpower programming or econometric analysis. The break provides an opportunity for reflection and for resetting personal goals. It sometimes can lead to a change in career direction, or a departure from government service entirely.

Certainly, most university programs force managers to exercise their intellects in a concentrated way. The longer time period permits such concentration to be focused on a specific project or subject which may be far more demanding and complex than a short-term training program can deal with. The fellowship can also be a reward in itself, letting a government executive know that he is on his way up and that his career development is valuable to the government.

Policy regarding these fellowship deals has been obscure, and there is little wonder that questions have been raised about costs and benefits. The government may pay some $40,000 for a year of graduate training for an executive (salary, tuition, moving expenses, etc.). If the study is merely decompression from 20 years of service, how can its value be measured? Then it has been discovered that executives are given this reward for such reasons as:

1. Moving a man out of a key job for partisan purposes where Civil Service regulations would otherwise forbid it
2. Keeping a man "on ice" for a year during reorganization
3. Providing relief for an executive saddled with an incompetent underling he can neither transfer nor fire

The fellowship system can be rationalized to some degree by implementation of the Intergovernmental Personnel Act. In the meantime, it simply points up the lack of a federal executive development system.

Techniques are less important than the systematic view and the clarity of objectives. *Who* does the training is of critical importance as well. The question at the beginning of a new decade still remains: Will the public services adopt a developmental strategy?

11. Leadership Development in the '70s

Speaking in 1967, Roger Jones set forth a number of imperatives for the Civil Service Commission in the field of career development and training. Jones has had a distinguished career in government, including service as Civil Service Commissioner and then Assistant Director of the Bureau of the Budget. He stated the needs as follows:

1. A system for evaluating career development programs
2. Defining and delimiting the kinds of training which best can be done by the federal government to meet its own needs and those of state and local entities
3. Determining the capability and willingness of academic institutions to undertake short-term, specialized training–as opposed to longer term "horizon-broadening" education
4. Developing a hard-core catalog of management skills needed by government executives to improve their performance
5. More money for training, which "should be accompanied by the conviction that training is a component of all personal services appropriations. . ." (Quoted in Golombiewski and Cohen, p. 307.)

The extraordinary element in this five-item list is not a lack of sense or substance; it is the fact that perhaps the leading personnel man in government should be admitting to such a primitive status for the craft.

It might not be totally unjustified to elaborate, a few years later, on the continuing needs, since the Jones agenda is still open. The order is changed to make the argument more timely for the 1970s.

The Knowledge

Despite a general American suspicion about research in human behavior, especially when it has political potential, a significant research task remains to be done. What management skills do we expect government executives to have? When names are fed into the partially computerized executive selection system John Macy developed for President Johnson and Harry Flemming reprogrammed for President Nixon, what variables make the difference?

To be more specific, the President's Council for Urban Affairs should sponsor a major research project in leadership for public service at all levels. The members of such an august group as might include Secretaries of Labor, Commerce, HEW, HUD, Transportation, and the Director of the Office of Economic Opportunity should have better information on what it takes to run a federal bureau, a state highway department or a Model Cities program. How can situational variables be altered to maximize a manager's chances for success? What can each level of leadership provide to bring about that maximization?

The Council for Urban Affairs might give the Urban Institute or some other uncluttered operation the dollars and get a useful product. Or the new White House Office of Management and Budget might take the challenge as its own.

The Evaluation System

Once there is *some* agreement on needs, the next step is not program but an agreed upon system for evaluating results. If government at any level is to proceed with leadership development activities, it must have the kind of measuring system which will give its experimentation duration and scope. The wheel is invented every day in training. A strong evaluation system can lead to a more efficient allocation of scarce resources. And no matter what happens, training resources promise to be extremely scarce in the 1970s.

The evaluation system will have to deal with many seeming incompatibilities: organizational goals and personal mobility, institution-building and professionalism, upgrading of minorities and technical expertise. The human intelligence can deal with these variables, and should.

For this evaluation task, the Civil Service Commission might contract with a major private or semi-public contractor, stipulating, of course, that the evaluation system be created by an integrated team (blacks, women, young people)—not just the white technocrats who normally do the major management consulting and thinking for the federal government.

A starting point for the study might be a review of existing evaluation systems development. Greenleigh Associates did a good beginning study for the Office of Economic Opportunity two years ago. HEW has a great deal of information available. Occasionally, management development contractors have left reports, and these can be dug out of files.

The Technological Assessment

After the evaluation system has been devised, at least a quick variant must be applied to the current management development technology. *What* kind of training system works for what reason on what kind of manager? Where and when and how and why does a government agency use the managerial grid? sensitivity training? management games? hortatory motivational techniques? case studies and other classroom devices?

After the *what* has been evaluated—at least so that the traditional form of codifying and freezing knowledge, the government manual, can be prepared—the next step will be to focus on the *who*. The scarcity of training resources will be apparent. Where does one go to have in-house trainers developed? Can client-oriented sources of service be found? Are there universities which can be induced to provide the service? Will private outfits do it based on an agency's needs rather than their own product? Can experiments and demonstrations be structured so that the results become useful at all levels of government?

The task of technology assessment probably calls for an intergovernmental task force. There is little expertise among the government departments most concerned. Among the federal departments of Labor, Commerce, Housing and Urban Development and the Office of Economic Opportunity, there are probably not a half-dozen people who could serve on such a task force as experts. The project would require representatives from at least the following entities:

1. The States. California has done the most adequate work, but individuals from state governments with unusual records of achievement—New Jersey's Department of Transportation, for example—should also be helpful.

2. The Cities. The wasteland is vast, but there are possibilities: some of the public health officers who have undergone training with the U.S. Conference of Mayors, the City of Detroit's personnel operation, and individuals from New York and Los Angeles departments which have used extensive outside training services.

3. County or Regional Entities. The Port of New York Authority probably has one of the best training systems—public, private or mixed—in the country. Miami-Dade County and Tennessee Valley Authority personnel could offer different perspectives. Indianapolis and Richmond managers might bring the concept of merger theory, up to now only thought of among big businesses, into the public staff development picture.

4. Relevant Nongovernmental Organizations. Major public employee associations and unions must be represented. The Scholarship and Education Defense Fund for Racial Equality (SEDFRE) is perhaps the only organization concerned with training and upgrading black elected and appointed municipal and county officials. The

American Association of University Women has developed a community leadership training program for women and has a strong staff. The New Jersey Community Action Training Institute has conducted and evaluated training for local human resources agencies around the country. The National Training Laboratories (NTL) have a network which includes some of the most perceptive individuals in the management development field. Some of the NTL network and most of the current recognized authorities in the field are affiliated with universities and can bring academic resources—from useful centers at the University of Michigan, Case-Western Reserve, MIT, Yale, UCLA and others—to bear upon this problem. Some other private training firms would appear to have special insight into the needs of the younger generation in today's public service.

The federal input into this state-of-the-art investigation begins with the Civil Service Commission. Since CSC is somewhat thin in management development expertise, the departments which have made the greatest use of training technology for their own management will have to participate. These departments include Air Force, Army, State, NASA, and, most recently, Post Office. Health, Education and Welfare should be involved not only because of its middle name, but because the National Institute of Mental Health has conducted serious research into training technology and the Social Security office has done useful training. The Internal Revenue Service, which has perhaps the most comprehensive training program, should also be involved.

How could such a technology assessment be put together? One temptation is to recommend a contract from the Civil Service Commission to the RAND Corporation or to NASA, for results. It would probably be more useful to have the Office of Management and Budget utilize the Advisory Committee on Intergovernmental Relations (ACIR) as the primary agency, in order to stress *intergovernmental effectiveness* rather than personnel functions.

The Demonstrations

A step that may be taken at the same time as the first three is the financing of a series of experimental projects in management development at various government levels. Such demonstrations should be designed to test various strategies and different delivery mechanisms. They should get more than the usual one-year project period. For most strategies two years should be an adequate test. Given the shortage of competent resources, there should be no hesitation to finance new (nonprofit) corporations to conduct the experiments. There have been a number of comparative tests in training under the war on poverty. OEO's Mid-Atlantic Region tested a variety of strategies using universities, private contractors and community-based nonprofit training organizations. The data was not collected systematically, however, and little useful evidence remains.

The Community Action Training Institute got more useful results in a community leadership training program during the early and more experimental days of the community action program. In an effort to prove that ghetto residents could provide useful adult education services in the ghetto, CATI developed a new careers experiment in the training of "adult education aides" and their use in service delivery, all within a one-year time frame. In an effort to test training resources, CATI divided the group of aides into three geographic segments and gave one segment each to a state university, a private training company and a community action agency. The evaluation standards were precise and based on job performance. (See Passett and Parker, pp. 16-20.)

Given the priority of government's labor-management relations, it might be useful to see experiments in training in that area contracted to major trade unions, both in and out of the government service fields. A good test would be the bringing together of labor and management negotiators for joint training in negotiating skills! Another possibility might be to have the American Arbitration Association conduct a demonstration.

The demonstrations most necessary at this stage in the development of "creative federalism" are those of leadership development in local and state agencies handling federal grants-in-aid. At the local level, programs involving the interaction among municipal government, citizen boards and federal grants are in need of help.

The Model Cities programs offer a particularly complex challenge to the training and development professional. The city staffs dealing with the complex programming needs of a model neighborhood need a broad spectrum of training services, as do representatives of state agencies dealing with the program. The Model Cities staff is often made up of a mix of white professionals and neighborhood leaders from various minority groups. Staff development services can help build an organization, reduce the usually frenetic turnover, and help personnel relate better to the community they serve. Skills training for staff is essential in planning, programming, grantsmanship, budgeting, fiscal management, community organization and a host of specialized program areas.

Perhaps the most innovative role for a training strategy, however, comes in the provision of services to Model Cities citizen policy and planning committees. Citizen participation, the key method of the 1960s for politicizing the poor and disenfranchised, has been a difficult process to implement in Model Cities. (See Cahn and Passett pp. 236-269.) The neighborhood leadership tends to display severe role conflicts, an inability to function effectively as a group and weak policy-making (or advising) skills. They are not paid; the amount of time involved is substantial, as are the frustrations in dealing with government. The process often moves to the more standard ward-level politics: a job here, an "honest" hand in the till there. A training strategy would involve a new reward system for citizen leaders: a free comprehensive program of skills upgrading on an individual basis and group building for the board. The quality will have to be high and provide significant motivation to be worth the upwards of eight hours a week of effort it will require of the participants. The program will make a substantial investment in the development of its own leaders—and they, in turn, will both run the programs more effectively and provide themselves with career opportunities. (Such an experiment may be conducted by Systems for Change, Inc., in the South Bronx in 1971.)

Tests at the local and state levels are most important. The Civil Service Commission and federal operating agencies might do even more sophisticated demonstrations at the Washington level. Ever since the now famous management improvement project at the State Department (described by Argyris), students of various schools of human relations training have been arguing what-might-have-been. Why not tests of managerial grid, unstructured T-group, TRW-style organization development, the more elaborate learning games, programmed instruction, case method and even standard classroom techniques? The results would be of extraordinary value to the educational and industrial systems as well as to all levels of government. And this time the Ford Foundation should be given a respite— the government can finance its own training.

The Programs

The key program initiatives should emerge from the demonstrations, as well as from a catalog of needs and from the closed loop evaluation system. A number are already apparent from any analysis of government's workings. Some have been outlined in the preceding chapters. Here are more specific examples:

1. At the federal level, executives in key positions related to policy need an intensive orientation before they face the in-basket. Such an orientation should focus on the "possibles" in the job the executive is undertaking. The team providing orientation should include past holders of the job or of similar positions. Also involved should be counterparts from other agencies. Federal executives should be exposed to "the plunge" to get first-hand experience with the human results their programs are achieving. That experience must be integrated into a program of training and planning which impinges directly on the official's work day. In that way, his learnings on the block can be translated into day to day operational actions.

2. At the state level, newly appointed executives should receive classroom training on exploitation of federal resources—financial, technical, political. Such training involves role play and case study activity, as well as carefully structured confrontation with appropriate federal officials.

3. At the local level, a similar process might operate, vis-à-vis state and federal sources. Local officials also need extensive work on how to sort out the complexities of the local political scene: case work and classroom discussion on ethnic, religious, class, geographical and other divisions; the fiscal parameters of the government's programs; the ways public opinion is mobilized. They also can use even more basic work on systems such as PERT and PPBS. And they need practical labor—management relations programs, with intensive role play and case experience.

The Dollars

While the demonstrations are being implemented, the problem of money for human development in government should be resolved.

Roger Jones stated the conviction that training ought to be a component of all personal services appropriations. The characteristic of temporary systems in American life and the new striving toward higher "quality of life" make training the next fringe benefit. It will be the first fringe benefit based on Theory Y. It will probably be a step toward *one* civil service for public employees in America.

Many organizations are already allocating large portions of their budget to training—or to the effects of lack of training. One place where the "military/industrial complex" has had a great advantage over the domestic people-oriented programs, ironically, has been in the area of training expenditures.

Over the past 30 years, government has accepted a large number of costs in the personnel category which did not exist before. Pension plans and health insurance are two significant and relatively fixed charges which were adopted with much fuss and time-lag. The next fixed charge should be for training. A portion of every agency's personnel budget should be added for training each year. If the charge were generally applied, each agency might develop its own strategy to meet its own priorities. Logically, it should then compute its training budget. While that more systematic approach does not appear to lead to effective results now, it is still worth experimenting with and evaluating.

How much should be allocated to training? The suggestion here is to start with 10 percent of the personal services budget of every civilian federal agency, and its grantees, with a three-year authorization, and work from there. Hopefully, state and local governments will move to join the parade after a while. Those working at the state and local levels in federal grant-in-aid programs will be receiving the benefit from the first round, providing some effective pressure in that direction. The amount of money generated for developmental activities in the first year under this proposal might rise perilously close to $3 billion. Of course we cannot afford it. Just as we could not afford to raise policemen's pay—up over 50 percent in many large cities in the last few years since police union militancy began. Just as we could not afford adequate prices for health services —prices, which, with government subsidies aiding the cost push, are rising perhaps 30 percent a year. And just as we could not afford an increase in the price of public university education or an SST or a modest ABM system.

The priority is there. The need for a more effective and efficient public service is there. The recommendation makes sense.

Yet we have learned from other programs in the past decade— Medicare and Medicaid particularly—that placing an effective demand out front of needed professional human services does not mean that the quality services can be built and delivered on a time schedule. Moon landings, yes; medical services for all Americans, no. A substantial investment in training will overstrain resources, will it not? It will not strain the resources unduly if we have identified our needs, set up an evaluation system, tested a number of delivery models and have a clear dollar commitment a couple of years down the road.

Once an agency has a fixed pool of resources and each employee "owns" a piece of that fringe benefit, appropriate internal mechanisms should go to work. Top management will have a key planning and decisional input, aided by staff in charge of training and development services whose prestige should be enhanced in proportion to the increased resources at their disposal. Employee unions and other groupings should have a say over allocations and vehicles for human development. Legislative bodies should develop more interest in such activities and oversee them more carefully.

Once again, this is demand-push administration. While human resources do not exist to provide effective training for one major federal agency or a single state's public service, the supply can be created through the normal chaotic market principles which have applied as the nation has refused to tolerate scarcities in other specialties.

Fortunately, the Medicare model need not be followed. There, the hyper-professionalization in medicine and the peculiar politics of the professional organizations continued to squeeze supply even after demand became overwhelming. In the training field, provided the new system is not captured immediately by the professional educators, no such political strength and accompanying exclusionary structures exist.

New agents can be activated: the hundreds of new community colleges around the country which now do almost nothing in public service training; private companies already in the field and looking for the profits in expansion (particularly *some* of those reorienting from defense and space); the better of the new nonprofit institutions dealing with the demonstration; and perhaps even some universities. If young people and innner-city residents are indeed adept at human relations activities—as the evidence of Peace Corps. VISTA and economic opportunity programs might indicate—a whole new growth industry is theirs for the making.

The community colleges offer a particularly fertile opportunity for institutional growth to meet the need. They have not yet defined their roles in community service. They are accessible to pressure by local and county officials. They need not develop the academic pretensions which even extension divisions of universities seem to require. The buying of services by governmental units in fairly regular patterns can relieve the colleges' fiscal uncertainties.

Quality control will remain a major problem, but the catalog of skills and the evaluation system should assure that incompetence is not institutionalized—as it is now at all levels of public education from kindergarten to the doctoral level.

The program is not terribly complex. The need has been articulated in many places over the past 20 years. There have been piecemeal attempts to deal with the "leadership gap" and the "management gap" in public service. But there has been no coherent or consistent effort that would speak to the human development needs of people in government. There has been scandalously little effort of any kind to integrate and develop the new employee in public service—the young, the women, the blacks, the urban ethnics.*

Such efforts are presaged in the Intergovernmental Cooperation Act and in the Intergovernmental Personnel Act.** But their implementation at adequate funding levels will create a new public service, a public service which no longer runs on the model of an inefficient factory. A human development system in government will demand growth, effectiveness, and goal-achievement. "Window men" will no longer be able to function in their accustomed role.*** People in developmental programs will have lower tolerance for vague objectives, weak management, poor supervisors and paper pushing. Especially at the local level, they will probably be less constricted and secretive, seek out more participation, and be more open to new ideas and ways of doing things.

* And this at a time when the National Industrial Conference Board reports that one out of three technician jobs in medical research, air and water pollution, space and urban renewal is going unfilled because of lack of trained personnel.

** A version of the Intergovernmental Personnel Act was passed by both Houses in the dying hours of the 91st Congress and went to the President for signature as this book went to press.

***A window man, according to a congressman (recently retired) who wanted to place one in an agency the author was administering, is "You know, the guy in every government office; you put him by the window—he should look out and not bother anyone."

Implementation of the proposals here would not set up a national system of development and training. Federal agencies, and state, regional and local entities would develop their own programs, with assistance and sometimes participation at the various levels from civil service systems and central offices concerned with management improvement. Many training functions might be centralized or even instrumented over a period of time for the sake of quality and efficiency. Some programs would remain highly individualized. New institutions would be encouraged, and old institutions with particular capabilities would be utilized. The situation wherein a large number of people who should be running public programs may be training others to run them will have to be faced. The political and institutional problems affecting any idea which has not had significant public exposure and may not have a national major constituency are also real. There is no panacea here—just an idea and a program. It may take the decade of the '70s to bring it about. One can be confident that it will happen, however. Public servants will not let this decade go by before they apply "quality of life" standards to their working days.

more and better roads, recreation facilities, hospitals and programs for safeguarding the economic and social security of their being.

The major burden for providing these public services rests with our States and local governments. But, as these demands have mushroomed, their capacity to meet them has not. This is especially the case in terms of the numbers of qualified administrative, professional and technical personnel needed by State and local governments to plan, organize and administer the wide variety of programs authorized by past Congresses.

Between 1955 and 1965, State and local government employment increased from 4.7 million to 7.7 million persons. It is estimated that this total will increase to 11.4 million by 1975. Total recruiting needs for these employees, other than for teachers, are estimated at 2.5 million over the 10-year period, or an average of 250,000 per year. This, just to stay abreast of replacement and growth needs.

Nothing similar to this critical manpower situation has ever been faced by State and local governments before. There can be little question, that now and in the future, State and local governments face a serious problem of obtaining and retaining large numbers of high quality personnel. There can be no question that the general shortage of such trained and talented people throughout the country will compound this problem.

S.11 is intended to help strength State and local governments in their efforts to recruit and train personnel to meet these needs. It is almost identical with the bill (S.699) which passed the Senate in the 90th Congress by a substantial majority. House action did not take place and the measure died with adjournment.

Hearings were held on March 24, 25, and 26, and the bill was approved by the subcommittee on May 6, 1969. Favorable action was subsequently taken by the Committee on Government Operations.

The proposed legislation has now been considered in three Congresses. We have delayed much too long in dealing with the critical shortage of properly qualified personnel for the public service. Since the great expansion of public programs that occurred during the depression thirties, government has been chronically deficient in manpower. I quote from the report of the Commission of Inquiry on Public Service Personnel issued in 1933:

In spite of the vital importance of government and governmental services, American national, State, and local governments do not at the present time attract to their service their full share of men and women of capacity and character. This is due primarily to our delay in adjusting our attitudes, institutions and public personnel policies to fit social and economic changes of the past seventy years.

Mr. President, this should be revised to read "the past 100 years," for three and a half decades have passed and we have still not taken the obviously needed steps.

Such conditions are deplorable from any point of view, but they are intolerable when we consider that the vast programs of Federal aid, costing in excess of $20 billion annually, are largely dependent upon State and local governments for their execution. The burden grows constantly. S.11 is intended to help strengthen State and local governments in their quest for improved administration of these many programs and providing for meeting their responsibilities within the federal system.

Mr. MUNDT. Mr. President, S.11 reported by the Government Operations Committe was considered by the Intergovernmental Relations Subcommittee in this Congress and in the 90th Congress.

There has never been any divergence of view that the purposes of this bill for improving personnel administration in State and local governments were needed to meet the growing demands placed on State and local governments for governmental services. This bill authorizes the Civil Service Commission to make grants to these governments for carrying out training programs of its employees, for inclusion of State and local employees in existing Federal training programs, and to provide fellowships for university and college graduate training.

Mr. RIBICOFF. Mr. President, increasing demands for effective services are being made upon State and local governments across the country. The inability of local government to respond to these demands is becoming critical and should be of great concern to the Congress.

The Federal Government has helped expand State and local government programs without doing anything comparable to develop their professional, administrative, and technical capabilities.

If we are to appropriate billions of dollars each year to solve the problems confronting the Nation, it is surely sensible to spend a relatively small sum to insure that these programs will be properly administered.

The Government Operations Committee has now reported out S.11, the Intergovernmental Personnel act of 1969. This act is a meaningful first step toward developing effective State and local governments. As a member of the Subcommittee on Intergovernmental Relations, I am pleased to cosponsor this legislation.

S.11 is a comprehensive, carefully constructed approach to the problems of governmental efficiency.

The growth rates of State and local governments have been phenomenal. The number of Federal civilian employees rose from 2.4 million in 1946 to 3 million in October 1967—a 25-percent hike. On the other hand, State and local employee figures jumped in number from 3.6 million in 1946 to 9 million in 1967—an incredible 150 percent leap. Total recruiting needs for administrative, professional, and technical personnel at the local level are now estimated at 250,000 a year, and rapidly growing.

Linked with these developments has been an increase in intergovernmental assistance programs. Federal aid to States and localities amounted to $1.8 billion in 1948, and is expected to reach $25 billion for fiscal year 1970, a 1,290-percent increase.

Expanded Federal assistance has aggravated personnel problems at the local government level. Federal programs have moved local government into new and complex areas and programs which have seriously challenged the knowledge and competence of present employees.

James Sundquist and David Davis of the Brookings Institution have described the situation well in "Making Federalism Work":

> The irreversible nature of the changes wrought in the Federal system in the past decade gives special urgency to the administrative problems of federalism. While the Federal government will set objectives and allocate marginal resources available for new government programs to achieve the objective, it cannot administer the programs directly in most cases—and should not, even if it could . . . Administration, perforce, is thrust upon the state and local governments through grant-in-aid programs of various types.

Existing local resources simply do not permit long-range plans for training programs and other personnel services. Recruiting programs are generally feeble, underfinanced, and unsuccessful. Perhaps no greater problem faces local government today than that of attracting and retaining an adequate number of competent employees.

According to a survey conducted by the Public Personnel Association, little more than half of the 346 local government personnel agencies covered gave any attention at all to employee training. The amounts budgeted for this activity were small, commonly ranging from 2 to 10 percent of the total personnel agency budget.

What we now have is an ineffective and piecemeal approach for Federal training and technical assistance efforts. Most programs now relate to the needs of specific grants and to the specific State and local personnel administering them. Neglected has been the overall workings of central personnel management and training, which give local government its day-to-day thrust and capacity.

There is now talk of even greater decentralization of Federal programs. State and local governments should have more responsibility for making their own decisions about program priorities and then administering these same programs. Implementing such proposals will be disastrous, however, if we are not concerned at the same time with the qualifications, abilities, and training of the local government employees who are to run these new programs.

Bibliography

The bibliography is presented in this simple, annotated form to make it easily useful. The author assumes that the reader is familiar with the basic management training and organization development library—the works of Argyris, Bennis, Blake, Bradford, Likert, Lewin, McGregor, Marrow, Rogers, Schein, Watson and others. The sources here are those directly or indirectly utilized and referred to in the text.

The ERIC Clearinghouse on Adult Education at Syracuse University provided valuable help in the discovery of sources.

Books

Bass, Bernard M. *Leadership, Psychology and Organizational Behavior*. New York: Harper and Row, 1960. Contains a good catalog of leadership development strategies and methods.

Beckhard, R. *Organization Development: Strategy and Models*. Reading, Mass: Addison-Wesley, 1969. A brief manual of contemporary theory in the field, apparently written with an industrial audience in mind.

Bennis, W. and Slater, P. *The Temporary Society*. New York: Harper and Row, 1968. Critical theoretical background for the book's thesis on leadership development.

Bernstein, M. H. *The Job of the Federal Executive*. Washington: Brookings Institution, 1958. A Brookings study mainly concerned with recruitment and structure rather than with development and training. Useful with Corson for "state-of-the-art."

Bierenbaum, W. *Overlive: Power, Poverty and the University*. New York: Dell, 1969. The author's view of a university better geared into the society at large; holds great promise for training and development for public service.

Blake, R. R. and Mouton, J. *Building a Dynamic Corporation Through Grid Organization Development*. Reading, Mass: Addison-Wesley, 1969. A brief and hortatory book on the subject.

_____. *The Managerial Grid*. Houston: Gulf Publishing Co., 1964. The basic work on the system.

Blau, Peter M. *Bureaucracy in Modern Society*. New York: Random House, 1956.

Bolino, August. *Manpower and the City*. New York: Schenkman, 1969. An attempt to pull together the education, training, employment and transportation elements in the disparate manpower programs of the 1960s.

Cahn, E. F. and Passett, B. A., eds. *Citizen Participation: Effecting Community Change*. New York: Praeger, 1971 (replacing New York: Community Action Training Institute, 1969 and 1970 editions). Cases and analyses in various modes of participatory democracy in the late 1960s.

Caplow, Theodore. *Principles of Organization*. New York: Harcourt, Brace and World, 1964

Cleaveland, F. N., *et.al. Congress and Urban Problems*. Washington: Brookings Institution, 1969. The cases here provide a blueprint (and specific engineers, too) for the process which will have to be undertaken if the thesis of this book is to become policy.

Corson, John J. *Executives for the Federal Service: A Program For Action in Time of Crisis*. New York: Columbia University Press, 1952. Written in the McCarthy era and at the beginning of the Eisenhower administration, this book called for a strong public policy and public relations orientation on the part of new federal executives.

_____ and Paul, R. S. *Men Near the Top: Filling Key Posts in the Federal Service*. Baltimore: John S. Hopkins Press, 1966. An updating and expansion of the 1952 work.

Craig, R. L. and Bittel, C. R., eds. *Training and Development Handbook*. New York: McGraw Hill Book Co. (for American Society for Training and Development), 1967. A source book for training techniques.

Dahl, R. A. *Who Governs?*. New Haven: Yale University Press, 1961. A landmark study in the background of political leaders and the meaning of governmental leadership.

Galbraith, J. K. *The New Industrial State*. Boston: Houghton-Mifflin, 1967. Note last chapters on sociology of leadership.

Gardner, John. *Excellence*. New York: Harper and Row, 1961. A thoughtful book that is required reading for peculiarly American definitions of leadership.

_____. *Self-Renewal*. New York: Harper and Row, 1963. Stresses education and development for innovation. Chapter 8 discusses "organizing for renewal."

Ginzberg, Eli and Reilly, E.W. *Effecting Change in Large Organizations*. New York: Columbia University Press, 1957. An early study which Ginzberg and his colleagues have followed, with a strong human orientation.

Glazer, N. and Moynihan, D. P. *Beyond the Melting Pot*. Cambridge, Mass: MIT Press, 1963. The standard on "ethnics."

Golembiewski, Robert and Cohen, Michael. *People in Public Service*. Itasca, Ill: Peacock, 1970. Useful source book pulling together a variety of fugitive materials.

Guest, Robert H. *Organizational Change: The Effect of Successful Leadership*. Homewood, Ill: Irwin-Dorsey, 1962. Analysis of change in productivity after change in leadership in an industrial plant.

Herzberg, F. *Work and the Nature of Man*. Cleveland: World, 1966. Job enrichment defined in its broadest context.

Johnson. B. L. *Islands of Innovation Expanding*. Beverly Hills: Glencoe Press, 1969. The positive results of a survey of community college innovation around the country; not many relate directly to public service.

Katz, D. and Kahn, R. *The Social Psychology of Organizations*. New York: Wiley, 1966. A seminal book to be read in conjunction with Bennis' work.

Kepner, J. and Tregoe, B. *The Rational Manager*. New York: McGraw Hill, 1965. A rational problem-solving and decision-making system for industrial managers is easily adapted for productive use in government.

Lippitt, Gordon. *Organizational Renewal*. New York: Appleton, 1969. The organizational development strategy in an easy to read and easy to follow format; most of the focus is on industry.

Marris, P. and Rein, M. *Dilemmas of Social Reform*. London: Atherton, 1967. Focuses on various community strategies but does not deal directly with training as one.

Marrow, A. J., et.al. *Management by Participation*. New York: Harper and Row, 1967. A brilliant study on "how it's done" in industry.

McGregor, Douglas. *The Human Side of Enterprise*. New York: McGraw Hill, 1960. A landmark.

Molitor, Andre. *The University Teacher of Social Sciences and Public Administration*. Geneva: UNESCO, 1959. An early and strong call for more "administrative science" university study for public servants.

Nadler, Leonard. *Developing Human Resources*. Houston: Gulf Publishing Co., 1971. The first book in this series and important reading for conceptual orientation.

Nylen, Donald, *et.al.*, eds. *Handbook of Staff Development and Human Relations*. Washington: National Training Institute for Applied Behaviorial Science.

Pagano, Jules. *Education in the Peace Corps*. Brookline, Mass: Center for the Study of Liberal Education for Adults, Boston University, 1966 The former Peace Corps Director of Training describes that agency's system in a brief and highly readable paperback.

Passett, Barry A. *Staff Development*. New York: Educational Design, Inc., 1970. Packaged course for community agencies; contains manuals and tapes.

Rice, A. K. *Productivity and Social Organization*. London: Tavistock Publications, 1958.

Riggenberg, Clayton. *Local Government Training Programs, Problems and Needs in Iowa*. Iowa City: Iowa University, Institute of Public Affairs, 1968.

Romani, John H. and Raphaeli, Nimrod, eds. *Changing Dimensions in Public Administration*. Ann Arbor: Institute of Public Administration, University of Michigan, 1962.

Selznick, P. *Leadership in Administration*. New York: Harper, 1957. Though dated now, a most useful source on where the public service has been.

Smith, R. M., Aker, G. F. and Kidd, J. R., eds. *Handbook of Adult Education*. New York: The MacMillan Co., 1970. Extraordinary for its lack of relevance to this subject. (The most useful reference to public service training is in Nadler's chapter on "Business and Industry".)

Spiegel, Hans, ed. *Citizen Participation in Urban Development*, Vol. I and II. Washington: National Training Laboratory Institute, 1968. The articles on training development are weaker than their companions in the more substantive chapters on participation in the urban development process.

Stanley, D. J. *Professional Employees for the City of New York*. Washington, D.C: Brookings Institution, 1963. More a recruitment than a development strategy.

Stone, Donald C., ed. *Education in Public Administration*. Brussels: International Institute of Administrative Sciences, 1963. An international forum.

Sundquist, James L. *Politics and Policy*. Washington: The Brookings Institution, 1968. Critical background on "people programs" of the 1960's.

Tannenbaum, R., Wechsler, I. and Massarih, F. *Leadership and Organization*. New York: McGraw Hill Book Co., 1961.

Trist, E. C., et.al. *Organizational Choice*. London: Tavistock, 1963. The focus is on "response autonomy" and the use of therapeutic techniques to improve work group organization.

Wolfbein, S. *Education and Training for Full Employment*. New York: Columbia University Press, 1967. A decalogue of training with many useful ideas for enriching the working lives of public employees, by a veteran in the field.

Articles and Reports

Ackerman, Leonard. "Role and Organizational Location of Employee Development Specialists in the Federal Government." *Training and Development Journal,* October 1969, pp. 4-11.

Argyris, Chris. "Some Causes of Organizational Ineffectiveness Within the Department of State." *Center for International Systems Research*, Occasional Paper #2, 1967.

Bailey, Stephen K. "Education for Responsible Citizenship," NEA *Journal*, May 1965, pp. 16-18.

Benne, Kenneth D. "Authority in Education." *Harvard Educational Review*, August 1970, pp. 385-410.

Bennis, W. "Post-Bureaucratic Leadership." *Trans-Action*, July 1969, pp. 44-51 *passim*.

Bertcher, H. and Garvin, C. *Staff Development in Social Welfare Agencies*. Institute proceedings, Ann Arbor: Campus Publishers, 1969. Written primarily for social workers in manual form, these proceedings provide a useful reference for staff development in other public program areas.

Campbell, J. P. and Dunnette, M. D. "Effectiveness of T-Group Experiences in Managerial Training and Development." *Psychological Bulletin*, August 1968, pp. 73-104.

Cassel, Russell N. "New Dimensions of Leadership" *Adult Leadership*, April 1969, pp. 427-28.

Committee on Economic Development. *Improving Executive Management in the Federal Government.* Washington: GPO, 1964. As in Bernstein, the focus is on recruitment and restructuring of the federal personnel establishment.

Cone, William F. "Management Development: The Need for an Eclectic Approach." *Training and Development Journal*, September 1970, pp. 26-30.

Decker, C. E. *Employee Training and Development: A Study of Training Operations Under the Government Employees Training Act of 1958, with Special Reference to the Department of the Navy 1958-1962.* (Ph.D. thesis) Washington: The American University, 1963.

Deppe, D. A. and Obst, M. J., eds. *The University in Urban Community Service.* College Park: Center of Adult Education, University of Maryland, 1969.

Ferman, Louis A., sp. ed. "Evaluating the War on Poverty." *The Annals*, September 1969. Background information on OEO programs.

George, Alexander L. "Political Leadership and Social Change in American Cities." *Daedalus*, Fall 1968, pp. 1194-1217. Notes the key roles of great mayors of the decade.

Harlem Youth Opportunities Unlimited (HARYOU). *Youth in the Ghetto: A Study of the Consequences of Powerlessness and a Blueprint for Change.* New York: 1964. Amazingly, the creative "community action institute" concept gets short shrift in the published version of this innovative plan.

Hersey, Paul and Blanchard, K. H. "Life Cycle Theory of Leadership." *Training and Development Journal*, May, 1969, pp. 26-34. There is no single normative (best) style of leadership.

House, Robert J. "Leadership Training: Some Dysfunctional Consequences." *Administrative Science Quarterly*, March 1968, pp. 556-571. A warning that supervisors must follow-up to reinforce the positive learned behavior after training—or else the training may just cause conflict and reduced motivation on the job.

Ink, D. A. "A Management Crisis for the New President: People Programs." *Public Administrative Review*, November/December 1968, pp. 546-552. A strong statement written just before President Nixon was elected focused on management improvement in the federal system and particularly on a stronger role for the Bureau of the Budget, where Ink works.

International City Management Association. *Post-Entry Training in the Local Public Service.* Washington: GPO, 1963.

Jones, Victor, ed. *Proceedings of Conference on Continuing Education for Public Administrators in State, County and City Government in California, 1963.* Berkeley: Institute of Governmental Studies of University of California, 1965. Extremely useful, sophisticated presentations on the problems of leadership development.

Lindsay, Franklin A. "Managerial Innovation and the Cities." *Daedalus*, Fall 1968, pp. 1218-1230. Almost a sermon on the need to apply business school training methods to turn out thousands of generalist managers to deal with the problems of the cities.

Miller, S. M. and Rein, M. "Participation, Poverty and Administration." *Public Administration Review*, January/February 1969, pp. 15-25. Miller and Rein point out that the participation theme has had a significant impact on public administration and that public administrators have to change the way their bureaucracies operate in order to improve efficiency and increase participation at the same time.

Moan, C. E., Jr. *Public Employee Training on the State Level in the U.S.* Kingston, R. I: Bureau of Government Research, University of Rhode Island, 1964. Mainly concerned with paucity of data in the field.

Moyinhan, D. P. "What is Community Action?" *The Public Interest*, Fall, 1966.

Nadler, Leonard. "Training Directors and the War on Poverty." *Training Directors' Journal*, June 1965, pp. 34-40.

Passett, B. A. and Parker, G. M. *New Careers in Action*. Trenton: N. J. Community Action Training Institute, 1969.

Rogers, David. "The Failure of Inner City Schools: A Crisis of Management and Service Delivery." *Educational Technology*, September 1970, pp. 27-32.

Rustow, Dankwart, et. al. "Philosophers and Kings—Studies in Leadership." *Daedalus*, Summer 1968. A variety of perceptions on political leadership, with a strong focus on charisma and relatively little on management.

Sviridoff, Mitchell. "Contradictions in Community Action." *Psychiatry and Social Science Review*, October 1968, pp. 2-7. Useful overview of strategies for institutional change.

U.S. Congress, House, Subcommittee on Manpower and Civil Service of the Committee on Post Office and Civil Service. *Report Covering the Effectiveness of Implementation of the Government Employees Training Act of 1958*. 90th Congress, 1st Session, June, 1967.

U.S. Congress, Senate, Subcommittee on Intergovernmental Relations of the Committee on Government Operations. *Hearings on Proposed Intergovernmental Cooperation Act of 1965* (ICA). 89th Congress, 1st Session, April, 1965.

U.S. Congress, Senate, Committee on Government Operations. Subcommittee on Intergovernmental Relations. *Hearing and Report on Intergovernmental Personnel Act of 1969*. 91st Congress, 1st Session, April, 1969. A key source document with much significant testimony.

U.S. Government, Civil Service Commission. *Planning, Organizing and Evaluating Training Programs: Personnel Bibliography*. Washington: GPO, 1966.

————. Civil Service Commission. *Investment for Tomorrow*. A Report of the Presidential Task Force on Career Advancement. Washington: GPO, 1967. A sophisticated report on in-service training and education for federal employees.

————. Civil Service Commission. "Executive Preparation for Continuing Change." Addresses on the Dedication of the FEI, Charlottesville, Va: Federal Executive Institute, 1968.

128   Leadership Development for Public Service

_____ . Civil Service Commission. *Historical and Progress Report of the Federal Executive Institute*. Charlottesville, Va: FEI, 1969.

_____ . Office of Career Development, Civil Service Commission. *Interagency Training Programs*. Washington: GPO, 1968.

Weiner, Solomon. "Evaluation of the Professional Trainee Program." *Public Personnel Review*, October 1968, pp. 197-206.

Wood, Robert C. "When Government Works." *The Public Interest*, Winter 1970, pp. 39-52.

Index